HOW CHRIST CHANGED THE WORLD

HOW CHRIST CHANGED THE WORLD

THE SOCIAL PRINCIPLES OF THE CATHOLIC CHURCH

(*Formerly titled* **Christianity and Social Justice**)

By

Msgr. Luigi Civardi

Translated by

Sylvester Andriano

TAN BOOKS AND PUBLISHERS, INC.
Rockford, Illinois 61105

Nihil Obstat: Very Rev. Denis Doherty, S.T.B.
                    Censor Deputatus

Imprimatur: ✠ Aloysius J. Willinger, C.Ss.R., D.D.
                    Bishop of Monterey-Fresno
                    June 24, 1961

Originally published in English by The Academy Library Guild Press, Fresno, California, under the title *Christianity and Social Justice*.

ISBN: 0-89555-443-7

Library of Congress Catalog Card No.: 91-65350

Printed and bound in the United States of America.

TAN BOOKS AND PUBLISHERS, INC.
P. O. Box 424
Rockford, Illinois 61105
1991

"Then he saith to them: Render therefore to Caesar the things that are Caesar's; and to God, the things that are God's."

—*Matthew* 22:21

CONTENTS

TRANSLATOR'S FOREWORD

In the firmament of Catholic Action the name of Monsignor Luigi Civardi stands out as a star of the first magnitude. No one, it is safe to say, has done more to make known the mind of the Church on this all-important subject, to enlighten and inspire the faithful, and to spur them to action than Msgr. Civardi.

On April 17, 1911, he was ordained to the priesthood in Pavia, Italy, and two years later he received the degree of Doctor of Philosophy from the Academy of St. Thomas in Rome. His first appointment was as Diocesan Assistant to Young Men's Catholic Action groups in Pavia. At the same time he was teaching Catholic Action to students of theology in the Diocesan Seminary.

In 1924 he published his famous *Manual of Catholic Action* in two volumes, the first dealing with theory and the second with practice. This work has since gone through twelve editions and has been translated into sixteen languages. No book has contributed more to the spread of Catholic Action throughout the world. The publisher of the English edition is Sheed & Ward of New York.

In 1925 Msgr. Civardi was called to Rome by Pius XI, the Pope of Catholic Action, who appointed him Ecclesiastical Assistant for the Central Office of Italian-Catholic Action. As head of the Catholic Action Press he published the *Official Monthly Bulletin* of Italian-Catholic Action and from 1931 to 1947 he was also editor and publisher of a monthly Catholic Action review known as *The Ecclesiastical Assistant*. In 1934 there was founded in Rome "The Catholic Motion Picture Center," corresponding to our Legion of Decency, and Msgr. Civardi was appointed its first Director. While in charge of this office he published two works, *Motion Pictures and Catholics* and *Motion Pictures and Morals.* In 1944 Msgr. Civardi was appointed to the office of National Spiritual Director of the "Association of Italian Christian Workers," which office he held until 1955. Msgr. Civardi has been the soul of these Associations of Christian Workers, which played such a prominent part in the reconstruction of Italy after World War II and prevented the forces of Communism from dominating the Italian labor field.

In recognition of his valuable services Pope Pius XII in 1955 named Msgr. Civardi Director Emeritus of the "Associations of Italian Christian Workers" and appointed him a Canon of the Vatican Chapter. Since then he has made his residence in Vatican City, where he is continuing his writing.

Msgr. Civardi is the author of some thirty books, most of them on social questions. Of *Christianity and Social Justice* [now retitled *Handbook of Catholic Social Principles*], which I undertook to translate as a work of love, and which, thanks to the kindness of the Academy Guild Press is now appearing in print, one might apply the words found in Book III, Chapter 23 of the *Imitation of Christ:* "It is short in words but full of meaning and fruit."

Next to the social encyclicals and other pronouncements of the Popes, it would be hard to find a sounder, more authoritative or more succinct statement of the Catholic position on social questions than is to be found in this little work of Msgr. Civardi.

SYLVESTER ANDRIANO
Translator

San Francisco, California, May 11, 1961

INTRODUCTION

This book is written to serve as a text for Christian social education and training. Its primary purpose, therefore, is to set forth and explain some of the *social principles* contained in the pages of the Gospel and in those of the papal encyclicals that reflect the genuine light of the Gospel.

They are eternal principles because they issued from the mouth of Him who said: *"Heaven and earth shall pass, but my words shall not pass."* (*Matt.* 24:35).

They are the principles that should govern the lives of all peoples who glory in the title of Christian, no matter under what sky or in what social and political climate they may live.

But, we may be asked, is the Gospel then a social code?

To this question thinkers have given different and conflicting answers, hence not all true and exact, and so it is well that we know them before undertaking this study.

Around the debatable question concerning the *social value of the Gospel,* three currents of ideas have been formed. The first exaggerates this value, attributing to the divine Book a predominantly social content, and making of Christ above all a *reformer,* an *agitator*—almost a *forerunner* of modern revolutionaries. To this trend also belong certain humanitarian socialists like Pierre Proudhon.

The second current goes in the opposite direction in that it strips the Gospel teachings of all social content. The teachings of Christ, say its champions, have always soared in the lofty spheres of religion. His heavenly doctrines transcend every earthly system. On the other hand, history plainly tells us that Christianity may spring up and flourish in any political and social environment, adapting itself to such opposite forms of government as the aristocratic and democratic.

There is finally a middle course. It acknowledges that the Gospel is primarily a treasure of religious and moral truths, but affirms also its inestimable social value, because it contains fundamental norms and guiding lines for a safe journey over the slippery ground of political and economic life. This middle course is the true one. Once again, truth asserts itself between two opposite extremes.

The alleged religious transcendence of Christianity is indeed true, if by it we mean that the Gospel does not teach and does not lay down, *in a clear and explicit manner,* any political and economic system. But it is false, if by it we mean that every political or economic system is in equal harmony with the religious and moral principles of the Gospel.

We know that the Gospel is not a political, sociological or economic treatise and that consequently it does not put forward any kind of state constitution or socio-economic system. It is a code of supreme religous teaching and of unimpeachable moral principles.

But these moral principles are still fertile seeds that bring forth fruit in all fields of human life; they are unshakable foundations upon which the most beautiful social structures can be raised; they are premises pregnant with many practical conclusions that penetrate, by the power of dialectics, into the domain even of politics and of economics.

Therefore, even though we find in the Gospel neither the express condemnation nor the approval of definite political or social systems, we do, nevertheless, find those doctrinal elements and those ethical principles on the basis of which we are able to judge of their soundness or unsoundness; so that they may be said to be Christian or not, according to whether, viewed in their proper setting, they seem to agree or to disagree with the Gospel principles of justice and charity.

These statements find, or should find, a concrete and positive proof in the pages we offer, even though by reason of their brevity the arguments cannot here be treated as exhaustively as both the subject matter and the purpose of the treatise might well warrant.

And, since this text is not only for private enjoyment, but also for social training, we have deemed it advisable to speak not only to the mind, but to the Christian will and heart as well.

In this connection we should also state that our intention was to present in these pages, together with the main *social principles* of the Gospel, its inestimable *social benefits*. We did this for two specific reasons: to stir up in the heart a keener sense of gratitude toward Our Lord, and also to make those who wish to be apostles of Christ better fitted to present Him to the people as the *Supreme Benefactor* and *Social Redeemer.*

In fact, Jesus has ransomed us not only for the future life, but also for the present life. Christ has endowed us with riches for Heaven and for earth. He was the defender of all the oppressed and the persecuted, the strengthener of all weakness, the reliever of all miseries. He cast upon the earth the leaven of a new civilization, which is rightly called Christian.

The famous philosopher Henri Bergson, although far removed from the Christian faith, confronted by the force of facts, was obliged to confess: "Everything that has been done in the world since the coming of Christ that is good, and all that will be done, will be done through the merits of Christianity."

In the Encyclical *Sertum Laetitiae,* Pius XII wrote

these remarkable words: "It is indeed true that religion has its laws and institutions for eternal happiness,
but it is undeniable that it endows life here below with
so many benefits that it could do no more even if the
principle reason for its existence was to make men
happy during the brief span of their earthly life.

"In spite of all that, our heart bleeds to have to admit
that many poor misguided souls hold up Christ and
His Church to the masses as enemies of the people
and of civilization."

It is the aim of this brief study to offer a few weapons
to slay that sacrilegious calumny.

We all feel that a new order is being born amidst
the throes of this terrible world conflict. Let it be our
hope and our aim that this new social order will bear
the imprint of the Gospel of Christ. For today, as yesterday, and as tomorrow, what St. Peter proclaimed before
the Sanhedrin is and will ever be true: "For there is
no other name under heaven given to men, whereby
we must be saved." (*Acts* 4:12).

THE AUTHOR

CHAPTER I

CHRISTIANITY AND THE FAMILY

Preliminary Notions

1. The Christian belongs to three distinct societies: *domestic, civil* and *religious.*

These three societies are not opposed to one another, but are mutually complementary, each one answering to particular needs of man. They should, therefore, live in perfect harmony, helping one another.

Domestic society, the *family,* takes precedence over the other societies. In fact, it was instituted by God Himself, in the Garden of Eden, when He proclaimed this law: "Wherefore a man shall leave father and mother and shall cleave to his wife: and they shall be two in one flesh." (*Gen.* 2:24).

The family is, therefore, a natural society, because it was founded by the Author of nature Himself. Moreover, it is *necessary* by reason of its end, which is the generation and the education of man.

2. The family has its *root* and its foundation in *marriage.* Marriage actually creates, sustains and gives life to the institution of the family, as the soul gives life to the body.

Marriage is directed to these essential ends: *the propagation of life,* and hence *the preservation of mankind* (principal end); *mutual help between the spouses* and the *quieting of concupiscence* (secondary ends).

Marriage is endowed with these three essential prerogatives: (a) *Unity,* by which one man is united to

1

one woman (*monogamy*). Therefore, *polyandry* (more than one man with one woman) and *polygamy* (more than one woman with one man) are to be condemned. (b) *Indissolubility*, by which the marriage contract is not temporary but permanent. Therefore, *divorce*, which is an arbitrary dissolution of the marriage contract, is to be condemned. (c) *Sanctity*, which derives from the holy end of marriage, namely the propagation of life. The spouses, by exercising their generative functions, become co-operators with God, the Creator, Himself.

These sacred features which God Himself impressed upon the family and upon marriage had become shamefully disfigured at the time of Christ, not only among pagans but even among the Jews. Jesus Christ reformed and restored the family, by redeeming *marriage, woman* and the *child*.

The Restoration of Marriage

At the time of Christ, marriage, among all nations, had lost its essential and original characteristics: *unity, indissolubility* and *sanctity*. It had lost its *unity* because the husband could have more than one wife; its *indissolubility*, because divorce was possible even upon the most trifling grounds; its *sanctity*, because marriage was considered a mere instrument of pleasure.

Divorce was so common among the Romans in latter times that the philosopher Seneca remarked that many women "might have reckoned their years, not from the number of consuls, but of husbands." (The consuls were changed every year.) And St. Jerome, in one of his letters, speaks of a woman who had buried her twenty-third husband. Polygamy and divorce were obviously the ruin of the family.

Even among the Jews there was the so-called *bill of divorce*, by which a husband could put away his wife, for any reason whatever.

3. Jesus Christ elevated marriage by restoring its

primitive *unity, indissolubility* and *sanctity.* One day the Pharisees asked Him: "Is it lawful for a man to put away his wife?" and Jesus answered: "Have you not read that he who made man from the beginning, made them male and female? and he said, 'For this cause shall a man shall leave father and mother and shall cleave to his wife, and they shall be two in one flesh'? Therefore, now, they are not two, but one flesh." (*Matt.* 19:4-5).

"WHAT THEREFORE GOD HATH JOINED TOGETHER, LET NO MAN PUT ASUNDER." (*Matt.* 19:6).

With these words, Jesus sanctions the unity of marriage. He says, in fact, that man "shall cleave to his *wife,*" not to his *wives*; and that they are no longer two, but one flesh—not three, four or more.

Still more clearly He sanctions *indissolubility* by stating that man "shall cleave to his wife" and states that such a union is willed by God; consequently, a man cannot break it; "let no man put asunder what God hath joined together." Jesus Christ, by that absolute statement, does not allow divorce for any cause.

He also restored to marriage its sanctity; furthermore, He raised the marriage contract to the highest degree of sanctity and of dignity by making it a Sacrament, and *"a great Sacrament,"* as St. Paul calls it, comparing the union of husband and wife to the union of Christ with the Church, His spouse. (*Eph.* 5:22-23).

The Church, like its Divine Founder, has always recognized, both in words and in fact, the capital importance of marriage, surrounding it with many laws and safeguards, in order to protect its natural prerogatives.

The Marquis Francesco Pacelli—who played such an important part in the negotiations for reconciliation between the Church and Italy—said in his discourse at the Social Week of Rome

(September, 1929): "The question of marriage was a most delicate one. At the very outset of the negotiations, Pope Pius XI told me that for him *marriage was one of the most important points,* and that the State had to acknowledge the civil effects of the Sacrament of marriage contracted according to the laws of the Church."

When this concession was obtained, the Pope himself had occasion to write that this "is such a great benefit that for it I would have sacrificed life itself." (Letter to Cardinal Pietro Gasparri, Secretary of State, June 30, 1929.)

The Church, throughout the centuries, has suffered strife, persecutions and injuries of every sort, in order to preserve the essential characteristics of marriage as established by Christ.

Henry VIII, King of England, desired to divorce Catherine of Aragon and put Anne Boleyn on the throne. To Pope Clement VII, who protested it, he cried out: "Either the divorce or schism!" But the Pope permitted the schism of a whole nation in order to preserve the sanctity of marriage.

Such was the conduct of the Church in defense of Christian marriage in similar cases throughout nineteen centuries. It considered marriage sacred and inviolable and the foundation of human society and civilization.

The Elevation of Woman

1. Polygamy and divorce enable us to understand clearly what position a woman held in pagan families at the time of Christ: a servant, a tool of man—a plaything of his passions.

Even by the learned, a woman was looked upon as a being inferior to man. Plato wrote that: "The souls of the wicked will be punished in their second generation in the body of a woman, and in the third, in that of a beast."

Ordinarily, the consent of a young woman was not required in marriage. Her father gave her to whom he wished, or whomever paid most for her.

Among some peoples, there were also laws that gave the husband absolute power over his wife: he could punish her at will, sell her as a slave or even put her to death.

2. The Divine Redeemer raised woman from this state

of degradation by restoring her primitive dignity as a *companion* of man, *like unto himself.* God, in fact, in creating the first woman, pronounced these precise words: "Let us make him a help like unto himself." (*Gen.* 2:18) *Like,* not *inferior.*

This elevation of woman was brought about in various ways:

(a) Jesus elevated her first of all by being born of a woman. St. Paul writes: "God sent his Son, *made of a woman.*" (*Gal.* 4:4) A woman made kindred to the Divinity in the most intimate manner! What an exaltation of the feminine sex!

The Roman liturgy sings this magnificent praise to the Virgin: *"Thou before astonished nature didst beget thy Holy Maker."*

Dante in his *Divine Comedy* re-echoed the same theme: "Thou art she who didst human nature so ennoble that its own Maker scorned not to become its making." (*Par.* 33:2-6)

The same poet was able to describe this singular woman: "Lowly and exalted more than any other creature."

All human nature was ennobled by Mary; but especially feminine nature, because she was proclaimed *"blessed among women."*

Who would still dare to say, after that exaltation of Mary, that woman is a being inferior to man?

(b) Jesus elevated woman by restoring the *unity, indissolubility* and *sanctity* of marriage, thus making her the queen of the home and enshrining her natural gifts, as it were, in an inviolable temple.

And yet St. Paul says: "Let women be subject to their husbands, as to the Lord; because the husband is head of the wife, as Christ is the head of the Church." (*Eph.* 5:22-23). But this happens only because of the need of authority and order in the family, which calls for unity of command. In fact, though subject to him, woman is always man's *companion,* not his *servant.* The Apostle, in fact, continues: "Husbands, love your wives, as Christ also loved the church, and delivered himself up for it. . . Let every one of you in particular love his wife as himself." (*Eph.* 5:25,33).

The power of the husband, therefore, has well-defined limits: he is the *head* of the wife, but for her welfare. He could not have a loftier Exemplar: Jesus Christ, who delivered Himself up for *His beloved spouse, the Church.*

On this point, Pius XI, in his Encyclical *Casti Connubii,* on Christian marriage, writes:

> This subjection, however, does not deny or take away the liberty which fully belongs to the woman both in view of her dignity as a human person, and in view of her most noble office as wife and mother and companion; nor does it bid her obey her husband's every request if not in harmony with right reason or with the dignity due; nor, in fine, does it imply that the wife should be put on a level with those persons who in the law are called minors, to whom it is not customary to allow free exercise of their rights on account of their lack of mature judgment, or of their ignorance of human affairs. But it forbids that exaggerated liberty which cares not for the good of the family; it forbids that in this body, which is the family, the heart be separated from the head to the great detriment of the whole body and the proximate danger of ruin. For if the man is the head, the woman is the heart, and as he occupies the chief place in ruling, so she may and ought to claim for herself the chief place in love.

(c) Jesus rehabilitated woman by making her *substantially equal to man:* equal with regard to the end (Heaven), the laws, the means of salvation, etc. In this connection St. Paul writes: "There is neither Jew nor Greek: there is neither bond nor free: *there is neither male nor female,* for you are all one in Christ Jesus." (*Gal.* 3:28).

Neither does the Church make any distinction between man and woman in the distribution of graces through the Sacraments, in the rites of beatification and canonization, in the cult of the saints, etc.

> How do the worldly minded look upon woman today? As in the pagan era: a creature destined to satisfy the lusts of man. In conversation, in romances, in novels, in illustrated reviews, on the stage, on the screen, woman is appreciated only on account of her exterior endowments, for her ability to gratify the less noble

instincts of man; a *female*, not a *woman*, nor a *lady*.

Indeed, except for the light of Christianity, woman is destined to lose her noble prerogatives, to abase herself and to become inferior to man, forced to serve him.

3. Man has specific duties toward woman:

(a) *Not to do anything to offend the virtue of the honor of woman;* nothing that we would not want done to our mother, our wife, or sister.

(b) *To have a high regard for woman;* not to look upon her as the pagans did; that is, as an inferior being, a plaything of man.

(c) *To defend the virtue and the honor of woman;* to uphold her in her weakness, to guide her, to correct her when necessary, so that she may not step down from her lofty station.

Medieval chivalry, inspired by Christianity, had among its precepts: "You will respect all weaknesses and you will constitute yourself a defender of them." We know that among the weaknesses to be respected and defended, woman held a prominent place.

In this sense, every Christian must also be a perfect knight; for his program calls for the *respect and the defense of woman.*

The Redemption of the Child

1. Outside the light of Christianity, the weak are destined to be neglected, if not despised and trampled upon. This explains the lot not only of woman, but also of the child.

In the pagan family, just as the husband had absolute power over his wife, so had the father absolute power over his children; he could punish them at will, abuse them, sell them as slaves, or even put them to death. The famous apologist Tertullian, in the second century, wrote against the persecutors of Christians as follows: "Amongst so many men who thirst for the blood of Christians, how many are there that have not put to death one or more of their children; that have not caused them to die of cold or of hunger or exposed them as prey to dogs?"

In Rome, at the height of its civilization, the child, as soon as he was born, was placed on the ground at the feet of his father; if the latter took him up into his arms, that meant that he acknowledged him as his own and consented to support him; on the other hand, if he left him on the ground, that meant that he rejected him and accordingly he was left exposed on the public streets and no one bothered with him anymore. Thus abandoned, the poor, unfortunate creature could encounter no other fate but to perish of hunger or of cold, or to be devoured by dogs. At times, however, a still more tragic lot awaited him, for there were concessionaires of beggary who had the right to take possession of the abandoned child and mutilate it, in order to exploit it later on by putting it out to beg alms from the public. (So writes L. Garriguet in his book on the social value of the Gospel.)

And does not the same thing happen today in some pagan countries?

2. Jesus has also lifted up this frailest of beings, the child, and He has done so in many ways:

(a) First of all, by becoming a child Himself, obedient to Joseph and Mary: *"He was subject to them."* (*Lk.* 2:51). "How can a Christian today fail to surround with regard and kindness this frail creature, if the Son of God Himself wished to put on such frailty? For the same reason, in the Christian family, *the children are not considered heavy burdens, but sweet pledges of love."* (Pius XII in the Encyclical *Sertum Laetitiae*).

(b) Jesus showed His predilection for children; He caressed them, blessed them, praised them, nay, more, He identified Himself with them by saying: "And he that shall receive one such little child in my name, receiveth me." (*Matt.* 18:5).

"And they brought to him young children, that he might touch them. And the disciples rebuked them that brought them. Whom when Jesus saw, he was much displeased, and saith to them: Suffer the little children to come unto me, and forbid them not; for such is the kingdom of God. Amen I say to you, whosoever shall not receive the kingdom of God as a little child, shall not enter into it. And embracing them, and laying his hands upon them, he blessed them." (*Mk.* 10:13-16).

No wonder, therefore, that the Church, heir to the spirit of Christ, has woven a marvelous net of educational and protective institutions for the benefit of childhood.

(c) St. Paul, after having exhorted children to obey their parents, adds: "And you, fathers, provoke not your children to anger, but bring them up in the discipline and correction of the Lord." (*Eph.* 6:4).

If the dignity of the child is so lofty, his education is the noblest of all arts and a most worthy action.

Some people ask, as if scandalized: "Why did Jesus Christ keep Himself in the seclusion of His home in Nazareth until He was thirty years old? Could He not have spent this time to better advantage?"

We have just learned some of the wise motives for such seclusion: The restoration of the family through the redemption of marriage, of woman, and of children. Should not this be enough to account for and to make us appreciate the long retreat of Nazareth?

We should be grateful to the Divine Redeemer because, by the sacrifice of His hidden life, He chose to bring so many blessings to family life and, indirectly, to social life as well, since the family is truly the *cell of society*.

CHAPTER II

CHRISTIANITY AND WORK

Preliminary Notions

1. Leo XIII, in his Encyclical *Rerum Novarum,* defined work as "human activity for the purpose of providing for the needs of life and especially for its preservation."

In the definition are set forth the essential characteristics of work, which is at once *personal* and *necessary.*

It is *personal* because it is activity of the *person,* an intelligent and free creature, superior to every other earthly creature. Hence, the *dignity* of labor cannot even remotely be compared in the productive field to any activity whatever, whether of animals or of mechanical instruments.

Moreover, work is *necessary* because it is ordained *"to provide for the needs of life."* After the sin of Adam, the earth, cursed by God, produced no more fruits without the painful labor of man. In fact, God said to sinful man: "Cursed is the earth in thy work; with labour and toil shalt thou eat thereof all the days of thy life." (*Gen.* 3:17). Thenceforth, work became a *necessity* and a *means of life* for man.

2. Unfortunately, the *dignity* and the *necessity* of work were misunderstood by man in the course of centuries. Christ also rehabilitated work and workmen. The latter owe everything to the Divine Redeemer; not merely goods of supernatural life, but also of natural life.

10

Let us consider this immense benefit by making a comparison between what work was in the *pagan world* and in the Hebrew world and what it has become in the *Christian world,* through the redemptive work of Christ, as illustrated by His example. Such a comparison will reveal to us the greatness of the benefit and our duty to give thanks.

Work in the Pagan and Hebrew World

We speak of *manual labor* as that which requires the exercise of physical energy.

In the pagan world, when Christ came upon earth, manual labor was both in *theory* and *practice* despised and looked upon as unworthy of a freeman.

1. IN THEORY

(a) The greatest philosophers—Plato, Aristotle, Cicero—although they were able to discover sublime truths by the power of their intellects, held this odious theory concerning manual labor: Plato teaches that workingmen must be deprived of all political rights. Aristotle considers work done by laborers "as degrading and contrary to virtue." Cicero writes that: "All trades of workingmen are to be considered contemptible, and that there is nothing lofty about the workshop."

(b) Such were the views not only of men of science, but also of religion. The historian Suetonius tells us that workingmen were excluded from the forum, along with the slaves, when the high pontiff offered sacrifice in Rome.

2. IN PRACTICE

(a) The practice was in keeping with the theory, if not worse.

Manual labor, and the mechanical arts in the vast Roman empire at the time of Christ, were practiced almost entirely by slaves, so that manual labor became equivalent to *servile labor,* i.e., *slave labor.*

Now, slaves were not regarded as *men* but as *beasts,* or, worse still, as *machines,* as *chattels.* They were subjected to the most exhausting labor without any remuneration. Their only compensation was a very coarse and scanty living, just enough to keep up their strength that it might be employed in new and endless toils.

(b) *The slave had no rights before the law.* He was the property of his master, who used him as he pleased. He could *hire* him out, or *sell* him to anyone, and even put him to death. Indeed, there were many citizens who hired out their slaves just as horses, beasts of burden and vehicles are hired out today.

History tells us of peeved mistresses who killed their hairdressing slave on the spot with a stilleto for the crime, true or fancied, of not having combed their hair to suit them. History relates a still more gruesome fact, that of slaves put to death and fed to pet fishes.

(c) *The slave was not even permitted to marry* or raise a family, or, rather, he could do so only if the humanity or the interests of his master permitted him. However, it was a marriage only in appearance; it was no more than a precarious union, dependent upon the will of the master, who could separate the spouses at his pleasure.

In fact, it happened that upon the death of the master, or because of other circumstances, the husband and wife were sold to two different buyers so that their separation was brought about by the contract.

Moreover, the union of two slaves was devoid of all dignity and of all safeguards. The Roman law declared explicitly that between slaves there could be no adultery—everyone was free to violate their contubernium, namely the tent in which the two slaves lived together. Accordingly, the wife of the slave could be abused by anybody and the husband would have no redress.

Furthermore, the offspring of slaves belonged to the master, like the fruits of trees and the young of domestic animals. Not infrequently, they were separated from their parents. "Can one who is a slave be a father?" asked Plautus, a contemporary poet. And another writer, Ulpian, relates that masters in order to encourage their slaves to work, would say to them: "Work, work hard and in my will I will direct my son to make a gift of your children to you."

Jesus Christ and Work

The rehabilitation of work was such a difficult undertaking that only the God-man could accomplish it. In fact, work was identified, as it were, with slavery, which was one of the main props of society and, therefore, deemed legitimate and necessary by the great philosophers mentioned above.

Jesus Christ achieved this great boon for mankind by His *doctrine* and His *example.*

1. BY HIS DOCTRINE

Work, in the Old Testament, among the Jews, was not something dishonorable, but a duty. In *Genesis* it is said that: "The Lord God took man, and put him in the paradise of pleasure, to dress it and to keep it." (*Gen.* 2:15).

Jesus restored this ancient doctrine to honor, and perfected it.

Above all, He rehabilitated the workingman, by preaching one Divine Fatherhood, the universal brotherhood of men, and the natural equality of all men. The patrician and the plebeian, the master and the workingman, although occupying different rungs in the social ladder, have to invoke the same *Father, who is in Heaven.* This doctrine lays the axe to the root of the evil tree of slavery by condemning every substantial difference between men.

Expounding the doctrine of the Master, St. Peter exclaims: "God is not a respecter of persons." (*Acts* 10:34). And St. Paul: "There is neither bond nor free." (*Gal.* 3:28).

2. BY HIS EXAMPLE

But the stupendous example of Christ proved to be even more efficacious than His teaching.

(a) The Son of God became "the carpenter's son" (*Matt.* 13:55). Furthermore, He, Himself became a carpenter, a fellow-worker of His foster father. The Evangelist Mark, tells us that when He preached for the first time in Nazareth, His native town, His fellow-citizens who had always seen Him at work in His shop: "And when the sabbath was come, he began to teach in the synagogue: and many hearing him were in admiration at his doctrine, saying: How came this man by all these things? and what wisdom is this that is given to him, and such mighty works as are wrought by his hands? Is not this the carpenter, the son of Mary. . .And they were scandalized in regard of him." (*Mk.* 6:2-3).

As has already been stated, some marvel that the Redeemer should have spent thirty years at the shop in Nazareth, because they believe that He could have employed those years to better advantage. They forget a great truth: In the shop of Nazareth began the greatest and most beneficial social revolution that the world has ever known: *The rehabilitation of work.* Such an undertaking, which wrenched one of the hinges off pagan society—slavery—was altogether too difficult to be accomplished by the preaching of a doctrine, no matter how sublime and authoritative. It needed the shock of a lofty example: that of the Man-God.

After Christ handled the axe and the saw, no workingman can ever again be the object of contempt. On the contrary, he will become the object of special consideration, for henceforth every workingman will be able to call Christ by the intimate name of *fellow-worker.* By his very trade, he will have a trait in common with the King of Heaven and earth.

(b) Jesus, after leaving the shop at Nazareth, started His public mission and immediately selected His *fellow-workers,* the Apostles. Whence did He pick them? Nearly all of them were from the ranks of workers. The first four of them—Peter, Andrew, James and John—were fishermen. We have here another condemnation of the current opinion that work was dishonorable.

The Evangelist Matthew thus describes for us the call of the two most prominent disciples: "And Jesus walking by the sea of Galilee, saw two brethren, Simon, who is called Peter, and his brother Andrew, casting a net into the sea (for they were fishers). And he saith to them, 'Come ye after me, and I will make you to be fishers of men.' And they immediately leaving their nets, followed him." (*Matt.* 4:18-20).

The Church and Work

Throughout the Christian centuries, the teachings and example of Christ brought about a profound and universal renewal of society. We will here mention very briefly what the Church has done for the rehabilitation of work and of workingmen, deferring the rest for the chapter on "Christianity and Social Justice."

1. In a society full of idlers, the Church taught from the outset that *work is a duty.* St. Paul, in his letter to the Christians of Thessalonica, wrote these significant words: "If any man will not work, neither let him eat." (*2 Thess.* 3:10).

One must not, however, exaggerate the meaning of these words. The Apostle of the Gentiles does not mean to speak solely of manual labor, but of any work, moral or intellectual, of *any occupation whatever that may in any way be truly useful to humanity.*

The commandment to work had already been given to the first man by God Himself, when He said: "In the sweat of thy face shalt thou eat bread." (*Gen.* 3:19). And through Adam, God was speaking to all men.

2. The Church taught that work is not only a *duty* but an *honor.* She always championed the *dignity of manual labor.* She constantly recalled, in a special way, the example of Christ and of the Apostles, and in that way she contributed to the *abolition of slavery,* which is one of her most notable social achievements.

The great Bishop of Constantinople, St. John Chrysostom, in a century when slavery still held sway, gave this advice to Christians: "When you see a man splitting wood or another enveloped in smoke, forging iron with a hammer, do not look down on him. Peter, with girded loins, drew the net, and worked as a fisherman after the Resurrection of the Lord. Paul, after traveling over so many lands and performing so many miracles, was sitting in his shop making tents while the angels were revering him and the demons trembling before him."

Under the inspiration of these striking examples, several Christians who belonged to the nobility became workingmen. The example of Crispin and Crispinian in the third century is well known. They belonged to a noble Roman family and had been brought up in idleness and luxury. After becoming Christians, they left Rome for France to preach Christianity. They settled in the city of Soissons, where they worked as shoe-makers.

3. The Church has always taught that work is not only a *means of support,* but also of *expiation* and of *sanctification.* It is a means of life, both *material* and *spiritual.*

Indeed, what is sanctity after all but the imitation of Christ, and how does Christ present Himself to us but in the garb of the workingman?

This is why St. Benedict, the father of monasticism in the West, lays down the monk's program in these words: *Ora et labora* (prayer and work). The monk must sanctify himself by these two means: prayer and work— work transformed into prayer.

Work can and should be a means of sanctification, even outside the walls of monasteries, for all workingmen. For no matter what the work may be, when it is done *with God* and *for God*—that is, in the grace of God and for the love of God—it always assumes the dignity of a rite and yields one kind of bread for this world and another for the next. The sweat of one's brow becomes sacred. The workshop is converted into a cloister.

4. In modern times the Church, through the voice of the Supreme Pontiffs, has more than once protested against the abuses of *capitalism,* which exploited labor by considering it as merchandise, to the detriment of

the dignity of the workingman. Leo XIII, in his Encyclical *Rerum Novarum,* writes: "Religion teaches the owner and the employer that their working people are not to be accounted their bondsmen; that in every man they must respect his dignity and worth as a man and as a Christian; that labor is not a thing to be ashamed of, if we lend ear to right reason and to Christian philosophy, but is an honorable calling, enabling man to sustain his life in a way upright and creditable; and that it is shameful and inhuman to treat men like chattels to make money by, or to look upon them merely as so much muscle or physical energy."

Following this up, Pius XI in the Encyclical *Quadragesimo Anno* deplored that employers treated "their employees like machines with no concern for their souls, indeed without giving a thought to their higher interests."

Pius XII in a discourse to the members of the Italian Christian Workers on May 14, 1953, recommended "the care of constant and practical human relations between employers and employees, between heads of departments and workers in industry" and warned them to consider "the workingman for what he really is: *Christ's brother and co-heir of Heaven.*"

Now how can a follower of Christ mistreat a brother of Christ?

Against the abuses of the capitalistic system, the Pontiffs likewise vindicated *the right to work.* In fact, as Leo XIII writes: "The preservation of life is the bounden duty of one and all, and to fail therein is a crime. It follows that each one has *a right to procure what is required in order to live"* (Enc. *Rerum Novarum*), and Pius XII in his broadcast commemorating the fiftieth anniversary of *Rerum Novarum* states: "To the personal duty of work imposed by nature, there follows the corresponding right of each individual to make the means of providing for his own livelihood as well as for that of his family."

Work, therefore, is something sacred, like life, for which it provides the means.

A practical and logical consequence of all this is the *gratitude of the workingman to Christ and to His Church*. The workingman has been doubly redeemed by Christ; for the future life and for the present life. If Christ had not come on earth, the workingman in all probability would today still find himself in the abject condition of pagan times.

Labor, therefore, can retain the conquests made in the Christian world and make new ones—as we trust—only if society will walk in the light of the teachings and example of Christ. Otherwise, labor is destined to sink once again into the abyss from which it has been lifted up.

CHAPTER III

CHRISTIANITY AND POVERTY

Preliminary Notions

Poverty is the condition of those who are more or less destitute of temporal goods.

There are different kinds of poverty.

1. It may be *absolute* or *relative.*

Absolute poverty is the condition of those who are destitute of all temporal goods, who lack the necessaries of life and therefore need the help of others. This condition is better known as *indigence, misery, beggary.*

Relative poverty is the condition of those who have no superfluous goods, having only what is strictly necessary for life. Such is the condition, for example, of an honest common laborer whose wages are barely sufficient to support himself and his family.

2. Poverty, both absolute and relative, may be *involuntary* or *voluntary.*

It is *involuntary* when it is due to extrinsic conditions, even if such conditions are accepted with perfect resignation.

It is *voluntary* when it is due to the spontaneous surrender of temporal goods. Such is the condition of religious persons who *take the vow of poverty* in order to be better able to cultivate the virtues and to attain evangelical perfection.

This condition of poverty is of *counsel,* not of precept.

One must also bear in mind that for Christianity, poverty is not a *state of perfection*, but simply *a means* of perfection. So that a poor man may be perfect or imperfect according to the use that he makes of his poverty.

3. It is also necessary to distinguish between *effective* and *affective* poverty.

Effective poverty is the actual lack of material goods, be it voluntary or involuntary.

Affective poverty (from affection) is the detachment of the heart from whatever wealth one may possess, be it little or great.

According to the teachings of Christianity, all have a duty to practice affective poverty because it is *necessary* to perfection; while effective poverty can only be recommended as a means, not necessary, but *useful* to Christian perfection.

The state of absolute poverty or penury is generally not advisable because it may easily become an occasion of sin and of debasement. To the faithful, the Church recommends relative poverty which excludes all superfluities, but not penury, because only in cases of a special vocation and consequently of special help from God can it become a means of perfection.

The Holy Spirit prompted this prayer to God:

"Give me neither beggary, nor riches; give me only the necessaries of life." (*Prov.* 30:8).

4. Jesus, who exalted the weak and raised up the oppressed, was not only the Redeemer of women, of children and of workers, but also of the poor. He so elevated poverty as to endow it with dignity. We will understand this better when we consider how the pagan world looked upon and treated poverty.

Poverty in Pagan Times

1. Before the time of Christ the poor were generally despised. Poverty was considered a state of inferiority, debasement and dishonor.

It is true that some ancient philosophers and some

oriental ascetics preached and practiced poverty. These, however, were exceptional cases or rather curious oddities, prompted by a selfish idea, namely by the desire not to have the worries that wealth brings with it. For if it be true that riches are desirable from many points of view, it is also true that they *are thorns*, as the Gospel tells us in the parable of the sower. (*Lk.* 8:14).

Sometimes poverty is the result of a haughty and extravagant spirit, despised and ridiculed by the people. Such was the case of those Greek philosophers who were branded with the name of *cynics*, which means in Greek "like dogs."

The most famous among these was Diogenes, who gave up even his little home in order to live in a barrel in the open country and who used to say: *"Omnia me mecum porto."* (I carry all my belongings with me.) Famous too was the philosopher Crates, who boasted that he used to go to bed at night without shutting the door, because there was nothing that thieves could steal.

2. The poor man, being despised, was naturally forgotten and left to shift for himself. Pity and kindliness toward the unfortunate and the poor were practically unknown in the pagan world. There were no almshouses, no shelters, no hospitals for the many ills of humanity.

The great number of slaves also shows us how the most absolute poverty was up to that time a very widespread as well as an incurable social plague—that plague that is known as *pauperism*.

A small favored class of rich men lorded it over the people: such is the dismal picture of the pagan world, so that the poet Lucan could truthfully write: *"The many live for the few."*

How Jesus Dignifies Poverty

After the coming of Jesus into the world, there is a complete reversal of values. Poverty is made honorable. It acquires a sacred character and is surrounded with help, with protection and veneration.

Jesus dignified poverty by *example* and by His *teachings.*

1. BY EXAMPLE

He is heralded King of Israel, but is born in a stable and lives as a poor workingman in the little home of Nazareth until He is thirty years of age. One day one of the scribes, having seen Him perform many miracles and thinking that by following Him he could acquire wealth and glory, says: "Master, I will follow thee wherever thou shalt go." But Jesus disillusions him at once by replying: "The foxes have holes, and the birds of the air nests: but the son of man hath not where to lay his head." (*Matt.* 8:19-20).

The poverty of Jesus reaches its climax on Calvary, where He is stripped of His garments, for which the soldiers cast lots. (*Matt.* 27:35).

Dante is right in stating that while the Mother of Christ remained beneath the Cross, poverty followed Him even upon the Cross: "...when Mary stayed below, poverty mounted the cross with Christ." (*Par.* 11:71-72).

Thus was poverty exalted to the highest degree by Christ; and after such exaltation what Christian would still despise it, or rather what Christian will not honor it?

The poor are more like Christ, therefore worthy of *greater respect.* Poverty for the Christian is a sacred thing. No wonder then if many, like St. Francis of Assisi, choose poverty as their *spouse.*

2. BY HIS TEACHINGS

Jesus *practiced* poverty first, then *preached* it. Here, too, He "began to do and to teach." (*Acts* 1:1). Here, too, His words receive power and strength from His conduct.

Jesus *exalts the poor; commands that they be helped; He identifies Himself with them.*

(a) *He exalts the poor.*

In the Old Testament, Christ is heralded as the

liberator of the poor: *"He shall deliver the poor from the mighty."* (*Ps.* 71:12).

He began His preaching by calling Himself He who is sent to "preach the gospel to the poor." (*Lk.* 4:18). He sets forth His program in the Sermon on the Mount, and His first words are these: "Blessed are the poor in spirit for theirs is the kingdom of heaven." (*Matt.* 5:3).

This phrase, *"poor in spirit,"* means *affective poverty,* which we have already mentioned. Therefore—as Father P. Marco Sales observes in his comments on the Gospel—the poor in spirit are "Not only those who, following the counsel of the Saviour, freely strip themselves of everything in order to follow Him, but also the poor in fact who bear their poverty with patience, and all those whose hearts are not set on riches and pomp, and who do not make their happiness consist in piling up wealth."

Later on Jesus confirmed His doctrine—strange to the ears of the world—with this famous parable:

"There was a certain rich man who was clothed in purple and fine linen, and feasted sumptuously every day. And there was a certain poor beggar, named Lazarus, who lay at his gate, full of sores, desiring to be filled with the crumbs that fell from the rich man's table. . .the dogs came and licked his sores. And it came to pass that the beggar died and was carried by the angels into Abraham's bosom. And the rich man also died: and he was buried in Hell. . ." (*Lk.* 16:19-22).

This parable is an exaltation of poverty, and at the same time the condemnation of wealth, as understood by paganism.

(b) But Jesus was not satisfied with exalting the poor, *He commanded that the poor be relieved.*

He said bluntly to the rich: "Give that which remains as alms." (*Lk.* 11:41).

One day a rich young man asked Him what he should do to obtain eternal life: Jesus gave him this advice: "If thou wilt be perfect, go sell what thou hast, and give to the poor, and thou shalt have treasure in heaven." (*Matt.* 19:21).

Another day He asked Zacheus to be His host. The

people wondered and whispered because Zacheus was a publican, a Shylock, a thief with gloves. But all wonder ceased when they heard the words of this publican addressed to his distinguished Guest: "Behold, Lord, the half of my goods I give to the poor; and if I have wronged any man of any thing, I restore him fourfold." (*Lk.* 19:8). Zacheus was well aware of Christ's predilection for the poor.

(c) Jesus did more: *He identified Himself with the poor.* On the day of the Last Judgment, He will speak these words to the elect: "Amen I say to you, as long as you did it to one of these my least brethren, you did it to me." (*Matt.* 25:40). Oh, the dignity of the poor! Hidden in him is the Lord Himself incognito!

History relates that the Lord sometimes revealed Himself in miraculous manner in the persons of the poor. We are all familiar with the celebrated incident in the life of St. Elizabeth, the wife of the Prince of Thuringia. She received a poor leper in her palace. She washed him, nursed him, anointed him, and bandaged his sores and made him recline on her princely bed. The incident was related to her husband who, enraged at his wife, entered the room to see if it was true, raised the bed covers...and saw the face of Christ, resplendent with light. He understood the miracle; repentant, he knelt to pray; then, turning to Elizabeth with tears in his eyes, kissed her.

The Church and the Poor

The Church, following the footsteps of Christ, has always *exalted and helped the poor.*

1. THE CHURCH EXALTED THE POOR

From the very beginning when paganism was at its peak, she has shown her predilection for the poor, rescuing them from universal contempt. She exalted the poorest among the poor—the slaves—deprived even of their natural liberty.

Here is a historical incident: Onesimus, a slave of Philomen, a wealthy Christian of Colossus, in order to avoid punishment at the hands of his master ran away to Rome and contacted St. Paul (who was then in prison). St. Paul converted him, baptized him and then sent him back to his master with a letter which is a sublime document of kindliness. He said: "I plead with thee for my own son, whom I have begotten in prison, for Onesimus. . .receive him no longer as a slave, but as a brother most dear. . .Welcome him as thou wouldst me. And if he did thee any injury or owes thee anything, charge it to me."

Therefore, the Christian master is bound to see in his slave, not merely a man, but a *brother,* and *a very dear one.* Slavery is conquered with a vengeance.

While slavery was in full force, masters and slaves, rich and poor, went together to the Eucharistic Table, where they received one and the same Bread—the sublime sign and at the same time the cause of spiritual brotherhood.

After the celebration of the Eucharistic Mysteries, it was the custom in Rome and elsewhere on solemn occasions to celebrate the *Agape* (fraternal banquet). And here, too, patricians and plebeians, rich and poor, used to sit at the same table, partaking of the same food.

Slaves were admitted, under certain conditions, even to the Sacrament of Holy Orders, so that during the sacred ceremonies one might see nobles bowing their heads to receive the blessing of a Bishop or a priest who, up to yesterday, had been a poor slave neglected and despised by the pagans.

2. THE CHURCH HELPED THE POOR

Imitating the example of the Redeemer, the Church has always had a special care for the poor and the needy. These, as Bossuet said, are *"her firstborn and authentic sons."*

(a) This care *began with the dawn of the Church.* The *Apostles,* in addition to their strictly religious functions, performed works of charity and relief—at first, personally, and later through the College of Deacons, who were commissioned *"to serve at the tables"* of the poor and of the widows. (*Acts* 6:1-4).

In those primitive times, in the Church of Jerusalem
. . ."the multitude of believers had but one heart and
one soul:. . . neither was there anyone needy among
them. For as many as were owners of lands or houses
sold them, and brought the price of the things they
sold and laid it down before the feet of the apostles,
and distribution was made to every one, according as
he had need." (*Acts* 4:32-35).

St. Paul, in his arduous apostolic travels, is engaged
in collecting alms for the poor of the famine-stricken
Churches of Judea. (*1 Cor.* 16:1-3).

(b) *Throughout the centuries* how many institutions of charity have sprung from the bosom of the
Church: Almshouses, old age shelters, institutions for
the handicapped, for the blind, for the deaf. . . it may
well be said that the history of the Church is the history of charity itself. The latest chapters of that history are adorned with the names of Cottolengo, Don
Bosco, Ozanam, Dom Guanella and Don Orioni.

(c) In fact it has always been the teaching and
the mind of the Church that charity should be not only
a contribution of money but of one's self: a charity that
ministers not only to the body but to the soul.

His Holiness Pope Pius XII says in this connection:
"The great temptation of an age that calls itself social,
in which—besides the Church—the State, the cities, and
other public bodies attend to many social problems,
is that persons, even among the faithful, when the poor
man knocks at their door, simply send him to the
Department, to the Office, to the Organization, figur-
ing that their personal obligation has been sufficiently
satisfied by their contribution to those institutions in
the form of assessment or donations.

"No doubt the needy person would then receive your
help in that other way. But often he counts on you,
at least on a word of kindness and of comfort from you.

Your charity must resemble God's, who came in person to bring us help."

Among the charitable institutions that sprang from the maternal bosom of the Church for the relief of the poor, the *Conferences of St. Vincent de Paul* are a typical example. They were founded in Paris in 1893 by Frederick Ozanam, who, after receiving Holy Communion, would visit the poor, saying: "I am going to return the visit to Jesus."

This two-thousand-year-old tradition of Christian charity has completely changed the opinion of the world concerning poverty. "The poor man," writes Cardinal Capacelatro, "amongst us is no longer a despised creature as he was nearly always in ancient times. Christianity has created the dignity and the nobility of the poor—Christ's brother—and ours. This sentiment has been so transfused into the blood of Christian nations nowadays that it is shared even by unbelievers, and none of them would dare to say to a poor man today: 'I despise you because you are poor.' "

CHAPTER IV

CHRISTIANITY AND RICHES

Preliminary Notions

1. The principles of Christianity concerning poverty set forth in the preceding chapter should be completed by the teachings of the Gospel concerning material goods and the use we should make of them.

God, the Creator, said to the first couple: "Fill the earth and subdue it; and rule over the fishes of the sea, and the fowls of the air and all living creatures." (*Gen.* 1:28).

The Psalmist sang of this dominion of man over the whole of nature with these expressions of gratitude to God. "Thou hast set him over the works of thy hands. Thou hast subjected all things under his feet, all sheep and oxen: moreover the beasts also of the fields. The birds of the air and the fishes of the sea that pass through the paths of the sea." (*Ps.* 8:7-9). Thus did God give to man the right to occupy the earth, to till it, to enjoy its fruits and to make the very animals serve his uses and needs. In sum, He gave him the right to use all material goods *as a means for the conservation of life.*

But material goods not only serve to satisfy the legitimate needs of life; they also serve to satisfy desires and to provide comforts and pleasures. That is why they are so easily abused by man.

2. *All men have the right to possess and to enjoy the goods necessary for life.*

The right to life, indeed, carries with it the right

to the possession of material goods. We will treat of this more fully in the following chapters. Here we should, however, point out that material goods are unevenly distributed. This accounts for the social phenomenon of poverty, which we have already examined, and the contrary phenomenon of wealth, which we are about to examine.

Wealth is the condition of those who possess abundant means, beyond what is sufficient for life. We also give the name wealth to the goods themselves that *produce wealth.*

How must we look upon wealth in the light of Christianity? What are the teachings of Christ and the Church concerning its use and its distribution?

These are questions which we propose to answer.

And in order to set forth more clearly the originality, the nobility and the benefit of the teachings of Christ on this subject, we will first consider how wealth was regarded and employed in the pagan world.

Riches in the Pagan World

1. Before Christ, the wealthy man could *use* and *misuse* his goods without any limitations and without any consideration for others. Even in the midst of starving people, he could destroy the wheat with which his granaries were bulging. Pity for the poor, help for the needy and almsgiving were generally unknown, neglected and often despised as acts of weakness.

Pagan philosophy and religion imposed no duty upon the rich toward the poor. Dives, gorging himself and letting Lazarus starve at his door (*Lk.* 16:19-31), is the type of the rich man in pagan times.

Such was the idea, and such the use of riches in the pagan world. *The greater the riches, the greater the reveling,* was the order of the day. And what of those who had nothing? "Let us not speak of them, but look and pass." (*Inf. 3:51*).

2. Consequently, in those days there were a few immensely wealthy men, living in luxury, surrounded by an immense crowd of poor suffering people. The writers of those times describe the fabulous riches of the Roman patricians—numerous mansions and villas with all sorts of luxuries, lands and rich furnishings without limit.

A wealthy Roman possessed hundreds of garments. The poet Horace tells us that Lucullus—celebrated for his sumptuous banquets, known as Lucullan—on one occasion loaned to a theatrical agent five thousand mantles which he kept in his wardrobe for family use, while in the poor quarters of Rome thousands upon thousands of poor wretches languished and shivered from cold.

And—horrible to say!—one of the chief items of the long list of assets of these owners was represented by human flesh, by men—chattels, slaves. The wealthy Roman owned thousands of them. The famous writer Pliny tells us that under Emperor Augustus, a rich landlord by the name if Isodor Sicilius, in spite of having lost a considerable portion of his wealth during the civil wars, still had 4,116 slaves when he died.

Jesus and Riches

The Divine Redeemer also heals this social sore of *Mammonism* (the cult of Mammon—the god of money).

He does *not condemn* riches; He proclaims *the dangers* of them; He teaches their proper use and points out the *advantages of such use*.

1. HE DOES NOT CONDEMN RICHES

One day a rich young man comes to Him and says: "Good Master, what good work shall I do that I may have life everlasting?" Jesus replies: "Keep the commandments." All that is necessary for salvation is to keep the commandments of God: one need not give up his goods.

But the young man insists: "All these I have kept...what is yet is wanting to me?" And Jesus answered: "If thou wilt be perfect, go sell what thou hast, and give to the poor, and thou shalt have treasure in heaven; and come follow me." (*Matt.* 19:16-21).

Therefore, whoever wishes to be perfect must not only keep the commandments but also strip himself of all his goods. This, however, is a *counsel,* not a *universal precept.* Jesus wanted His Apostles to abandon everything: home, their few belongings, wife and children, in order to follow Him. But among the disciples of Jesus during His apostolic travels, we find also some pious women, "who used to provide for them out of their means." (*Lk.* 8:1-3). To these He does not enjoin absolute poverty.

Lazarus of Bethany was rich, and yet Jesus calls him *friend. (Jn.* 11:11).

2. HE PROCLAIMS THE DANGERS OF RICHES

The Gospel tells us how that rich young man, upon the final proposal of Jesus, "went away sad, for he had great possessions." And the Divine Master then said to His disciples: "Amen, I say unto you, that a rich man shall hardly enter into the kingdom of heaven." (*Matt.* 19:22-23).

Riches make it *difficult* to enter the Kingdom of Heaven.

(a) Because by affording us many comforts here below, they more easily make us forget God and Heaven.

(b) Because they afford us many means of gratifying our most exigent and dangerous passions.

(c) Because they are likely to render us proud and covetous by making us neglect the grave duties that riches impose, as we shall see presently.

Here is how St. Paul, faithful interpreter of Christ's mind, comments on the advantages of poverty, contrasting them with the dangers of riches.

"But godliness with contentment is great gain. For we brought nothing into this world, and certainly we can carry nothing out; but having food and wherewith to be covered, with these we are content. For they that will become rich fall into temptation and into the snare of the devil, and into many unprofitable and hurtful desires, which drown men into destruction and perdition. For the desire of money is the root of all evils, which some coveting have erred from the faith, and have entangled themselves in many sorrows." (*1 Tim.* 6:6-10).

3. HE TEACHES THE PROPER USE OF RICHES

"*With difficulty,*" said Jesus, "*will a rich man enter the Kingdom of Heaven.*"

But *difficult* does not mean *impossible.* The rich man, too, therefore, *can* and *must* be saved. Indeed, he can attain the highest degree of perfection, making good use of his wealth. Among the saints, there were many rich men.

But in order to be saved, one must make *proper use* of riches. For that purpose Jesus teaches that it is necessary:

(a) *To keep one's heart detached from earthly goods,* that is to be poor *in spirit* if not *in fact.* The latter is required of a few, the former of all. "Blessed are the poor in spirit" (*Matt.* 5:3), said Our Lord: and poor *in spirit* are also the rich whose hearts are not attached to their riches.

Jesus said: "You cannot serve God and mammon" (namely riches). (*Matt.* 6:24). He did not say that one cannot *possess,* but that one cannot *serve* wealth. That is, we may not make a *master* or an *idol* of money, sacrificing everything to it, even our conscience. We may possess money without being possessed by it.

(b) *Before God we are to consider ourselves not as owners, but only as tenants of our goods.*

"Or what hast thou that thou hast not received?" asks the Apostle Paul. (*1 Cor.* 4:7). The absolute master of everything is God, who grants us *the use* of some of His goods. Of this use we must render Him a strict account: *"Give an account of thy stewardship."* (The Parable of the unjust steward: *Lk.* 16:1-8).

Now our heavenly Master wants us *to use His goods for our legitimate needs, not to gratify our passions.*

(c) Furthermore, *He wants us to give what is superfluous to the poor.*

Already the Precursor, foreshadowing the mind of Christ, had told the people of Israel: "He that hath two coats, let him give to him that hath none; and he that hath meat, let him do in like manner." (*Lk.* 3:11).

The Divine Redeemer is even more absolute with this precept of His: "Give that which remains as alms" (*Lk.* 11:41); in other words, that which is not necessary for the support of oneself and his family, *according to each one's social condition.*

On this point Leo XIII explains: "No one is obliged to distribute to others that which is required for his own needs and those of his household; nor even to give away what is reasonably required to keep up becomingly his condition in life; *'for no one ought to live in a manner that is not becoming.'* (St. Thomas). But, when *necessity* and *convenience* have been satisfied, it is our duty to give what is left over to the poor. It is not a duty of *justice*, except in cases of extreme necessity, but of *Christian charity."* (Encyclical *Rerum Novarum*).

Unjustly persecuted by the police, without a cent in his pocket, having given his last pennies to some starving beggars whom he met on the road, Renzo leaves his native town and goes to his cousin Bartolo to ask for help. "Very well, you may count on me. God has blessed me with goods that I may do good." (*The Betrothed,* Chap. 17). How much wisdom and Christian charity in those words! Everyone who has been favored with goods from God should repeat both in words and in fact: *"God has blessed me with goods that I may do good."*

The famous apologist Tertullian said that the *rich man was created to be God's treasurer upon earth.* Now when the rich man gets to be like that we can well speak of the *dignity of the rich,* as we have already spoken of the dignity of the poor.

4. HE POINTS OUT THE ADVANTAGES DERIVED FROM THE PROPER USE OF RICHES

Riches, far from being an evil, become an instrument of good, a source of merit, when rightly used. The benefits of their right use, and particularly of alms-giving are indeed many. Let us review some of them.

1. *The right use of riches opens the Kingdom of Heaven to us.*

Jesus, in fact, will say to the elect on the Day of Judgment: "Come, ye blessed of my Father, possess you the kingdom prepared for you from the foundation of the world; for I was hungry and you gave me to eat; I was thirsty and you gave me to drink." (*Matt.* 25:34-35). It is noteworthy that here Jesus identifies Himself with the poor.

These explicit words are also of Jesus: "Make unto you friends of the mammon of iniquity; that when you shall fail, they may receive you into everlasting dwellings." (*Lk.* 16:9).

2. *The right use of riches merits for us the help and blessings of God.*

Jesus said: "Give, and it shall be given to you..." (*Lk.* 6:38); you shall receive not in Heaven only, but also on earth, for God does not allow the charitable man to lack the necessities in life. The Holy Spirit says: "He that hath mercy on the poor, lendeth to the Lord." (*Prov.* 19:17).

And he who lends to the Lord, receives a very high rate of interest, and puts his money in a bank that never fails.

The widow of Sarephta says to the prophet Elias who asks her for food in the days of the great famine, because of the long drought: "I have no bread, but only a handful of meal in a pot, and a little oil in a cruse." Nevertheless, with the little that she had she prepared a cake, and from that day, through the special intervention of God, "the pot of meal wasted not and the cruse of oil was not diminished" till the rain came. (*3 Kgs.* 17).

How true the proverb: "You will never grow poor by giving alms."

The Teachings of the Church

1. The Church has always re-echoed the teachings of Christ concerning the use of temporal goods. She has never preached nor required perfect economic equality (ideally desirable and in keeping with the principles of human brotherhood) for the reason that such equality is practically impossible. Nevertheless, She has always condemned great inequalities that give rise to overabundance on the one hand and misery on the other. If the distances that separate the various social classes cannot be *eliminated,* they can at least be *shortened.* This is both possible and a duty.

Among the teachings of the Church on this subject, we will cite only two: one from the early days of Christianity and the other from modern times.

2. In the primitive Church it was the custom to hold *agapes,* or love feasts, in which all the faithful of every social class took part by mingling together the foods they brought with them (the rich more, the poor less) and all eating at a common table. However, at Corinth— as St. Paul tells us—instead of mingling their foods, each one brought and ate his own supper, so that it sometimes happened that the poor suffered hunger while the rich ate and drank more than necessary and even to excess. "One is hungry and another drinks overmuch," the Apostle complains, adding this severe reproach: "You despise the Church of God and put to shame the needy." (*1 Cor.* 11:20-22).

3. This sharp contrast between one who has too much and is wasteful and one who is without the necessities and suffers was accentuated in modern times by the capitalist system, giving rise to the so-called *distribu-*

tion and not of *production* of wealth.

Pius XII, in his broadcast referred to above, commemorating *Rerum Novarum,* categorically declared that *"the goods created by God for all men must be made available to all in an equitable manner, according to the principles of justice and charity."*

And he added: *"The economic wealth of a people does not properly consist of abundance of goods, but rather in a fair distribution of goods.* If such a fair distribution were not obtained or should be brought about only imperfectly, then the true end of national economy would be attained, for, no matter how helpful a fortunate abundance of available goods might be, the people, never having been called to share in them, would not be economically rich, but poor. On the contrary, see to it that such a fair distribution is actually brought about in a lasting way and you will see a people, even with smaller available resources, become and remain economically sound."

Pius XII championed an equitable distribution of goods, not only among individuals and social classes, but also among nations. He said: "In the field of a new order founded on moral principles, there is no room for narrow selfish calculations tending to hoard economic resources and materials, destined for the use of all, in such a way that nations less favored by nature are not permitted access to them."

Let us be thankful to the Divine Redeemer that among other blessings He also brought us this: *the right use of riches* for the salvation of the rich and for the relief of the poor. Let us bear in mind the teachings of St. Paul: "For we brought nothing into this world, and certainly we can take nothing out; but having food and wherewith to be covered, with these we are content." (*1 Tim.* 6:7-8).

And let us likewise impress upon our minds this teaching of Leo XIII: "God did not create us for these frail and perishable goods, but for the celestial and eternal, and the earth was given to us by Him as a place of exile and not as a fatherland. Whether you have riches or other earthly goods in abundance or whether you are deprived of them is of no importance as far as eternal happiness is concerned, but the good or bad use of those goods, that is supremely important."

CHAPTER V

CHRISTIANITY AND THE RIGHT OF PROPERTY

Preliminary Notions

1. The right of property is the *moral power to possess and to use a thing as one's own.*

This right is a corollary of *the right to live,* since it is impossible to live without the possession and the free use of definite material goods.

There are various kinds of property. The principal ones are:

(a) *Individual* or *personal* property when the owner is an individual or physical person; *collective* or *social,* when the owner is a community or a moral person.

(b) If it belongs to a *public community,* such as a State or the Church, collective property is called *public.* Otherwise it is private.

Private property, therefore, may be either individual or collective; in the latter case it belongs to a *private community,* like a corporation.

The State has the power to dispose of private property when the public interest requires it. For example, it can require the property of citizens for war purposes and by paying compensation it can condemn property to construct a road, erect a building, etc. . .

2. There are also other classes of property.

(a) *Productive property* that serves to produce other goods (for example, lands, factories, machines, raw materials, etc.); *consumer goods* that satisfy human needs (such as merchandise, furnishings, clothing, etc.).

(b) *Real property,* that is, immovable property (such as lands, mines, buildings) and *personal property* (to wit: merchandise, money, securities, etc.).

False Systems

1. Some regimes and systems, such as the *liberal system,* concede too much to the right of property, by failing to impose necessary limitations and obligations; other systems instead either deny such right or restrict it unduly. Such is the *communist system,* which advocates the communion of goods (hence its name).

There is *absolute communism* that insists upon the common ownership of all *goods, even of consumer goods.* Accordingly it denies every right of ownership. This utopian system is defended by the old-line communists, like Charles Fourier, who conceived the so-called *phalanstery* (large buildings in which citizens live a community life under the direction of the president, like the internes of a college). Today the trend is toward a *moderate communism* that attributes to the State (socializes) *only productive property.* Hence it does not insist upon the common ownership of consumer goods which may be privately owned.

2. What are we to say about the *socialization of productive goods,* which is such a major issue today?

The socialization—or nationalization—of the means of production and of exchange (lands, factories, commerce) may either be *total* or *partial.*

When socialization actually contributes to the *common good* it does not contravene the principles of Christian ethics on the subject of property. This should be our compass in this matter also.

Relying upon this fundamental principle, the sociologists in the Christian tradition acknowledge that a *partial* and *gradual socialization* (of the great means of production and of exchange) may be legitimate, provided it contributes to the welfare of the commu-

nity and not merely of a group. Expropriation is, of
course, contingent upon the payment of an *indemnity*.

Our Holy Father Pius XII confirmed this principle
in his message of March 11, 1945, to the *Christian
Association of Italian Workingmen,* in which he states
that one may consent "to socialization only in those
cases in which it seems really required by the common
good, that is to say, as the only truly effective means
of remedying an abuse or of preventing a waste of
productive forces of the country, to insure the organic
coordination of those same forces and to direct them
for the good of the economic welfare of the community,
so that the national economy in its normal and peaceful development may open the way to the material
prosperity of all the poeple, a prosperity such as will
at the same time likewise afford a solid foundation for
religious and cultural life."

The Right and the Use of Property

1. The Church, following the teachings of Jesus
Christ, has always taught that the right of private property is *natural,* that is to say established by the Author
of nature Himself, namely God. This is so for the following reasons:

(a) Because private property stimulates personal
interest which, in turn, *stimulates production.*

(b) Because the system of private property is more
apt to *guarantee the liberty and the dignity of man.*

(c) Because the just division of property *fosters
social peace,* while the community of goods easily gives
rise to quarrels and litigation.

These reasons seem contradicted by the fact that there are
communities—religious orders and congregations—in which the
communion of goods exists in the most perfect harmony and with
due regard for personal dignity.

One must bear in mind, however, that these communities exist
under peculiar conditions. First of all, every member has made

a *spontaneous surrender* of the right of personal property by embracing the state of voluntary poverty. In the second place, the members of these religious societies tend toward a *state of perfection,* for the attainment of which they have taken, in addition to the vow of poverty, the vows of obedience and chastity. In the third place, it is always a question of small societies in comparison with civil society. For these reasons their example cannot be urged in justification or as proof of the possibility of the communistic system which has to be realized under entirely different conditions and circumstances.

2. Nevertheless, the Church, having affirmed the right of private property as an essential factor and a condition of a *prosperous, well-ordered, respectable and peaceful life,* has always distinguished between the *right* and the *use* of private property, by teaching that even the natural law imposes *limitations upon the use of property.*

One must bear in mind two great truths in connection with this point:

(a) God alone, Creator and Bestower of every good, is the *absolute Owner* of all things, while men, with respect to Him, are nothing but *tenants and simple administrators* of them.

(b) God has created and bestows the goods of the earth that they may serve for the support of *all* men; since all have the duty and the right to live.

3. These two fundamental truths, naturally, give rise to several conclusions of the utmost practical importance.

(a) The first is this: the owner must use his goods *not as it pleases him, but as it pleases God,* to whom he must render an account of the use he made of them. Therefore, the definition of the right to property given by paganism: *ius utendi et abutendi:* the right to use and misuse, is false.

(b) God wishes the owner to use his property in such a way that, when his legitimate needs have been satisfied, *he should distribute the rest to the needy.*

(c) Property, therefore, has not only an *individual function,* insofar as it has to provide for the needs of the owner, but has also a *social function* insofar as it has to provide for the needs of other members of society.

This *social function,* moreover, is not merely a *counsel* but a *command,* a command of charity which, in certain cases, becomes a command of *justice.* We will now give a few proofs of these summary statements.

The Teachings of Christ

Jesus Christ has implicitly affirmed the right of property and its social functions.

1. In fact, He never condemned the ownership of private property, a thing He would certainly have done if such ownership was wrong or contrary to natural law.

But He did explicitly and emphatically condemn all abuses, both private and public, of His times and of His fellow citizens. He condemned phariseeism, false legal justice, pride, divorce, etc... How could He have failed to condemn property too if it were a theft, as it was called by the communist Proudhon?

On the contrary He affirmed, at least implicitly, on different occasions the right of private and individual property. Let us recall an episode already well known to us. The publican Zacheus says to Our Lord: "Behold, Lord, the half of my goods I give to the poor, and if I have wronged any man of any thing, I restore him fourfold." Jesus, approvingly, said to him: "Today salvation has come to this house, since he, too, [Zacheus] is a son of Abraham." (*Lk.* 19:8-9). Zacheus has thus obtained salvation by giving away half of his possessions, but not all. That means *that he had the right to own the other half.*

2. However, Jesus also affirmed the *social function* of property, by pointing out the duties of the owner toward others. And that was in contrast with the opinions of the teachers of Israel, who shared the pagan

idea of property which gave its owner unlimited power. Here are His plain and unequivocal words: "Nevertheless, give that which remains as alms." (*Lk*. 11:41). Jesus employs the imperative mood. Therefore, to give to the poor what is superfluous is a true precept. And that is superfluous—as we know—which is not necessary for the support of self and family, according to what is suitable to one's condition in life. (See preceding chapter).

Furthermore, the idea of the social function of property is implicit in the broader idea of *human brotherhood*, which is one of the chief points of Christ's message. Among good brothers, in fact, the cold words *mine* and *thine* lose their strict meaning, since one brother cannot feel satisfied if the other's stomach is empty.

3. The conduct of the first Christians of Jerusalem, while still under the spell of the words of Christ, is concrete proof of the teachings of Christ on this subject: "And the multitude of believers had but one heart and one soul: neither did any one say that aught of the things which he possessed was his own, *but all things were common unto them*. . . For neither was there any one needy among them. For as many as were owners of lands or houses sold them and brought the price of the things they sold and lay it at the feet of the Apostles, and distribution was made to each one, according as anyone had need." (*Acts* 4:32-35).

It should be noted, however, that this *communism* of the first Christians, the fruit of a great spirit of fraternal charity, was altogether *free* and *spontaneous*, and, since it was not imposed upon anyone, it was never practiced with strictness. This is evidenced by other statements of St. Luke himself. Take for instance the famous episode of Ananias and his wife, Sapphira, who brought St. Peter the money derived from the sale of a field that belonged to them, retaining, however, a part of the price for themselves. God punished them in a miraculous manner by causing their sudden death. What was the cause of the terrible punishment? Not because they had kept a part of the price, which they could have retained even in its entirety, but because they had lied and deceived the Apostle, to whom they had promised the whole price. This is very clear from Peter's reproach:

"Ananias, why hath Satan tempted thy heart, that thou shouldst lie to the Holy Ghost and by fraud keep part of the price of the land? Whilst it remained, did it not remain to thee? and after it was sold, was it not in thy power?...Thou hast not lied to men, but to God." (*Acts* 5:1-10).

The Teachings of the Church

The Church, too, while it has at all times proclaimed the right to private property, has also insisted upon the social function of property.

(a) *The teachings of the Apostles.*

St. Peter writes to the early Christians: "As every man hath received grace, ministering the same one to another." (*1 Peter* 4:10).

The Apostle is here speaking both of spiritual and material gifts.

St. Paul writes to his disciple Timothy as follows: "Charge the rich of this world...to do good, to be rich in good works, to give easily, to communicate to others." (*1 Tim.* 6:17-18).

(b) *The teachings of the Fathers and Doctors of the Church.*

The Angelic Doctor St. Thomas Aquinas, in his *Summa Theologica,* offers us this clear and precise teaching: "With respect to external goods man has two faculties, to wit: (a) the faculty of *procuring* and *distributing* these goods; for which reason it is lawful for man to possess these goods as his own (*right of property*), indeed, *it is necessary to human life...* (b) the faculty of *using* the goods themselves; and, *as far as their use is concerned, man ought to consider external goods not as his own, but as in common,* so that he may readily share them with those in need." (II-II, Question 66, Art. 2.).

All the Fathers of the Church have used very plain and forceful language on this point. Let this statement of St. Basil suffice: "We call him who strips another of his clothing a thief; why should we not apply a similar name to *him who does not clothe the naked when he is able to do so?* That bread which you are storing away belongs to the hungry; that suit which you are locking up in the closet belongs to the naked, those shoes which you are allowing to rot belong to the barefooted, and that money that you are hiding under the ground belongs to the poor. Therefore, *you are doing as many wrongs to your neighbor as the number of things that you could give him and withhold from him instead.*"

(c) *The teachings of the Pontiffs:*

Pius XI in *Quadragesimo Anno* writes:

"It follows from what we have termed the individual and at the same time social character of ownerships, that we must consider in this matter not only their own advantage but also the common good. To define these duties in detail, when necessity requires and the natural law has not done so, is the function of those in charge of the State. *Therefore public authority, under the guiding light always of the natural and divine law, can determine more accurately upon consideration of the true requirements of the common good, what is permitted and what is not permitted to owners in the use of their property.*"

Pius XI, in his Encyclical *Divini Redemptoris* (on atheistic communism) wrote: "The rich must not place their happiness in the things of this world, but considering themselves merely as administrators who know that they will have to render an account to their Supreme Lord, let them avail themselves of worldly things as precious means which God has placed in their hands to do good; and let them not neglect to distribute to the poor whatever is left over, according to the Gospel precept."

Pius XII in his radio broadcast commemorating *Rerum Novarum* stated: "*Without doubt, the natural order established by God requires also private property.*"

But this right of private property must not hinder *"the primary and fundamental right that grants its use to all men."*

A *primary and fundamental right* the Pontiff calls it, because the use of goods is necessary for the preservation of life, and the right to life comes before the right of property. So much so that—according to the teachings of Catholic morals—when a man finds himself in *extreme need,* he may take as much of his neighbor's goods as is necessary to keep from starving to death.

The same Pontiff (Pius XII) on another occasion said: "While the Church condemns every unjust violation of the right of private property, she admonishes, however, that it is *not* unlimited *nor absolute because it has precise social obligations."* (Address to the workers of Prote, Oct. 28, 1956.)

From all this it appears that Catholic teaching holds a position midway between the communistic doctrine, that would suppress every right of individual and private property, and the liberal doctrine that does not recognize its due limitations, thus justifying unjust inequalities.

Pius XI, in his Encyclical *Divini Redemptoris,* reminds us of this other truth: "Unjust disproportion of wealth in the economic field and vexing inequalities are one of the causes of the rapid spread of the communist idea in the world."

The *Fioretti of St. Francis,* Chapter XXI, tells us of "the wonderful miracle performed by St. Francis when he converted the ferocious wolf of Gubbio, which 'not only devoured animals but even men, so that the citizens were in great fear. . .' Francis, wishing to free the city from that scourge, goes forth to meet the beast and says to it: 'Brother wolf, I command you in the name of Christ not to do any harm either to me or to anyone else.' The wolf cast himself at his feet like a lamb and the Saint invited him to make peace with the people of Gubbio by telling him: 'I promise you that I will have the men of this town provide for you continually as long as you live so that you will not go hungry anymore, *for I know full well that it was on account of hunger that you did all the mischief.'* Thereafter, peace was actually made in the town square when the people, in the presence of St. Francis and the wolf, promised the latter 'to give him each day the things that he needed.' "

This charming Franciscan anecdote contains many lessons. Among others is this most timely one: All efforts to preserve social peace will avail little unless we see to it that the people, claiming their just rights, *"are given each day the things that they need."* This will, no doubt, be true when everybody will make use of the right of property in a Christian manner, as already explained.

CHAPTER VI

CHRISTIANITY AND SOCIAL JUSTICE

General Notions

1. Justice is the cardinal virtue *that prompts us to give everyone his due.*

According to its different objects, it assumes different names. Thus we have *commutative, legal* and *social* justice.

a) *Commutative justice* regulates the relations between one individual and another; for example, the relations between seller and buyer; the former must give sound and wholesome goods, the latter the just price agreed upon.

b) *Legal justice* governs the relations between rulers and subjects. The rulers have to enact just laws, and citizens have to observe them. It is legal justice also that inflicts penalties corresponding to the crimes, and in this case it is called punitive justice.

c) *Social justice* governs the relations between different social classes, between employers and employees, and distributes the benefits and burdens of society. *Fees, salaries* and *pensions* are the object of social justice, which is also called *distributive* justice.

2. *Justice is more compelling than charity in the sense that it has greater binding force.* The reason for this lies in the very nature of justice, which gives to others what belongs to them, what is due them *by strict right.* Hence, in justice, one does not give of one's own. Consequently, the exercise of justice at bottom is nothing

else than a reintegration of a restitution. Not so with charity, which gives to others what they are not strictly entitled to. In charity, one gives of one's own.

Our Lord illustrated this difference between justice and charity in the well-known parable of the vineyardists. (*Matt.* 20:16). To the first who went to work and labored all day, the owner gave the wages agreed upon and thus performed an act of social justice. To the last, who had done one hour's work, to the astonishment and envy of the others, he gave the same wages. We were here face to face with an act that goes beyond justice; here is a dash of generosity, an act of charity, for which Jesus does not want the owner reproached.

3. The first duty of charity to one's neighbor is this: *to do him justice, to give him what is due him.*

That is what Pius XI states in the Encyclical *Divini Redemptoris*, setting forth this principle: first, justice, then charity. *"The wage earner,"* he writes, *"is not to receive as alms what is his due in justice, and let no one attempt with trifling charitable donations to exempt himself from the great duties imposed by justice."*

And Pius XII in *Sertum Laetitiae* writes, *"If the rich and prosperous are obliged, out of ordinary motives of pity, to act generously toward the poor, their obligation is all the greater to do them justice."*

Unhappily, not all are of the same mind. There are some Catholics, even practical Catholics, who are much inclined to charity, but have not the same inclination toward social justice. They do indeed perform welfare works, but they underpay their employees. They do charity, but violate justice.

This is not true charity. To benefit, to give alms to one who has been exploited, is not to do a work of charity; it is, if anything, to make reparation to some extent for an injustice; it is a restoring of wages that have been withheld from their legitimate owner. No one can say that he is doing charity to a brother if he has not done him full justice first.

Teachings of Christ and the Apostles

1. Our Lord taught and defended every kind of justice and social justice in particular. In the Sermon on the

Mount He proclaimed: "Blessed are they that hunger after justice, for they shall have their fill." (*Matt.* 5:6).

Elsewhere He declares: "The labourer is worthy of his hire." (*Lk.* 10:7).

Jesus makes Himself a defender of justice, scourging the Scribes and the Pharisees, who, while pedantically observing religious precepts, disregard the inviolable rules of justice. Three days before His arrest He delivers a stinging rebuke to these self-righteous men: "Woe to you scribes and Pharisees, hypocrites: because you devour the houses of widows, praying long prayers. For this you shall receive the greater judgment. Woe to you scribes and Pharisees, hypocrites;...because you tithe mint and anise and cummin and have left the weightier things of the law; judgment and mercy and faith." (*Matt.* 23:14-23). Mark this phrase: *"the weightier things of the law,"* which shows the importance of justice.

2. The Apostles, too, were staunch defenders of social justice. We shall confine ourselves to two striking testimonies. St. Paul in his letter to the Colossians writes: "Masters, do to your servants that which is just and equal: knowing that you too have a master in heaven." (*Col.* 4:1).

If we bear in mind that in those days the servants were nearly all slaves and, consequently, considered and treated, not as men, but as beasts, as things, we will understand all the social value of this exhortation of the Apostle of the Gentiles.

Against employers who exploit the work of their dependents the Apostle St. James writes these very forceful words: "Go to now, ye rich men, weep and howl in your miseries, which shall come upon you. Your riches are corrupted: and your garments are motheaten. Your gold and silver is cankered: and the rust of them shall be for a testimony against you, and shall eat your flesh like fire. You have stored up to yourselves wrath against the last days. Behold the hire of the labourers, who have reaped down your fields, which by fraud has been kept back by you, crieth: and the cry of them hath entered into the ears of the Lord." (*James* 5:1-4).

The Catholic catechism teaches that to defraud workingmen of their wages is one of the four sins *that cry to God for vengeance* because it is positively contrary to the welfare of mankind, and therefore more deserving of divine punishment than the others.

What then shall we say of those who stir up hatred against the Church, picturing her to the workingmen as the friend and ally of exploiters of labor?

The Teaching and the Work of the Church

1. The Church did not limit itself to repeating the teachings of Christ and of the Apostles. She translated them into works for the benefit of the working class first of all, in order to safeguard the dignity of the worker. She strove for the abolition of slavery and later sought and pleaded for a just compensation for work. Thus it was that in the religious and social atmosphere created by the Church there arose in the Middle Ages the glorious *guilds of arts and crafts*.

They were associations of men exercising the same vocation, men who sought to safeguard not only their economic but also their political and social interests. They constituted a kind of hierarchy of labor, divided into three grades: *apprentices, journeymen* and *masters.*

The *apprentices* were young men learning the trade with a master, who kept them in his own house, supervised them and educated them with fatherly care, an admirable example of Christian fraternity.

The *journeymen* were accomplished laborers. They could not be dismissed, if the reasons were found to be inadequate by a special commission made up of journeymen. Evidently, here was a true labor court.

The *masters* were the heads of the shops and had to be distinguished for their religious, moral and technical qualifications. In order to prove their technical skill they presented a masterpiece.

Every year each corporation of carpenters, bricklayers, stonecutters, wool combers, merchants, druggists and physicians, of lawyers, just to mention a few, elected a head called *Consul* or *Captain.* He was assisted by minor officials whose duty it was to fix fair salaries and hours of work, to settle inevitable disputes, etc. . .

2. The guilds of arts and crafts were abolished by the liberals of the French Revolution in the year 1789 without substituting anything in their stead. They were abolished under the pretext of liberty, on the claim that the liberals wished to set up a system of *free competition* in the field of labor also.

The consequences soon made themselves felt. As soon as the restraints against the heartless speculations of the employers were removed and the laborers left in hopeless isolation, then the exploitation of labor on a vast scale set in. This evil was made still more unbearable by the gigantic strides of industry that swelled the profits of owners out of all proportions.

This gave rise to the *social question* looking toward the settlement of relations between capital and labor, between employers and employees.

The Supreme Pontiff Leo XIII, known as the *Pope of the Workingman,* dealt with it at length. As soon as he ascended the throne of Peter on February 20, 1878, he turned his gaze upon the wretched throng of workingmen and saw that—these were his exact words—"*a very small number of very wealthy men have imposed upon the vast multitude of proletarians a yoke that is little short of slavery.*" Deeply moved, he immediately took the part of the workingmen in order to free them from the new yoke fashioned by liberalism, the denier of Christ.

In fact, a few months after his election appeared the encyclical *Quod Apostolici Muneris,* in which the Pontiff issued the invitation to Catholics to "*support trade and labor unions.*"

Note the date: This encyclical was written on December 28, 1878, when very few concerned themselves with the working classes, and socialism, at least as an organization, was taking its initial steps. After that it may well be said that the Pontiff never omitted an opportunity to repeat this cry: *Go to the people, help the workingmen.*

3. His most solemn act, which remains indelibly carved in the pages of history, is his encyclical of May

15, 1891, which from its initial words is called *Rerum Novarum.* It deals with this specific subject, *"the condition of the working classes."*

This document condemns the *capitalistic system,* introduced by liberalism, because it overestimates the rights of *capital* and does not give just consideration to the rights of labor. He also reproves the socialistic system, which seeks the abolition of private property and class warfare, while Christianity is for the *collaboration of classes.*

The Pontiff then points out the economic, political and religious means for the solution of the social question. He reminds the rich and the owners that when *necessity* and *convenience have been supplied, it becomes a duty to give to the needy out of what remains over.* He reminds the governments of their duty to come to the aid of the workingmen *"with a whole set of laws and insititutions"* (for at that time governments followed the system of *laissez faire).*

But above all he pleads with Catholics of all nations to revive the ancient guilds, adapting them to present conditions: *"We see with pleasure,"* he writes, *"the formation of associations, whether they be workingmen only or of workingmen and owners, and it is necessary that they increase in number and efficiency."*

The wish of the *"Pontiff of the Workingmen"* was granted. His thrilling words caused many organizations and works on behalf of the proletariat to flourish in Italy and in other Catholic countries.

That great sociologist and Christian apostle, the late Giuseppe Toniolo, offset the appeal of Karl Marx, *"Proletarians of the whole world, unite!"* with this other appeal: *"Proletarians of the whole world, unite in Christ!"*

The professional Catholic organizations that had flourished throughout the whole world under the inspiring words of the Pontiff were later united in an *International Confederation* that was called the *White Confederation,* to distinguish it from the two *red* ones, that of the socialists and that of the communists.

4. In *Rerum Novarum* another question of vital importance finds its solution: The question of a just wage for work.

The wages of a workingman are in themselves something sacred because they represent bread, the staff of life, which is sacred. And yet liberalism left wages at the mercy of chance; it abandoned them to the gamble of freedom of contract between the owner and the workingman, and chance naturally was nearly always unfavorable to the weaker of the contracting parties: the workingman.

Leo XIII condemns this arrangement because it is opposed to justice. And he pens these plain and stern words: "The amount of remuneration must never be less than is necessary for the support of a frugal and well-behaved workingman."

Pius XI, in the encyclical *Quadragesimo Anno,* issued on the 40th anniversary of *Rerum Novarum,* goes a step further and proposes *"a family wage."* Here are his words, clear as crystal:

"The workingman is entitled to wages that will be adequate for the support of himself and his family."

And in the encyclical *Sertum Laetitiae,* Pius XII clinches the idea of a family wage when he writes: *"It is only fitting that the salaries of the workingmen be such as to suffice for themselves and their families."*

Cooperative Effort and Profit Sharing

1. Wages, however, is not the only method of compensation. Pius XI, in *Quadragesimo Anno,* offers another method still more progressive: *the participation in the profits of the business.* This form of compensation represents an integration and a corrective of wages.

On this point, too, the words of the Pontiff are very clear: "Wealth," he writes, "which has increased so abundantly during this century of 'industrialism,' as it is called, is not rightly distributed and equitably made available to the various classes of men. It is necessary that in the future the abundant fruits of production will not accrue unduly to those who are rich, and will be distributed with ample sufficiency among the workers."

In order that this may be more easily accomplished, the same Pontiff makes a concrete proposal by adding: "In the present social condition, we consider it more advisable, however, that, as far as possible, *the employment contract be somewhat modified by a partnership contract,* as is already being done in various ways, and with no small advantage to the workers themselves and to the owners. Workers and other employees thus become sharers in ownership or management and participate in some measure in the profits received."

Profit sharing is also advocated by Pius XII in his radio message of September 1, 1944, when he says: "Where a large concern continues to yield good returns, the employees should be *offered an opportunity of moderating the labor contract by means of a partnership contract.*"

In another pontifical document Pius XII calls for the "improvement of old fashioned formulas of remuneration and to make the workingman share more and more in the life, the responsibilities and the proportionate profits of the enterprise, also for the reason that often times they are required to expose themselves to grave risks in the field of labor." (Letter to the 39th Social Week of Italian Catholics).

2. In order to eliminate the exploitation of labor, Catholics always favored, moreover, a wise *cooperative system* which offers the great advantage of *uniting capital and labor in the same hands,* of breaking up excessive holdings without taking away the technical advantages of distributing the responsibility, and by augmenting the number of small owners. In fact, *cooper-*

atives of labor and *production* are partnerships in which their members are at once the owners and wage earners of the concern, dividing the profits in equal shares.

The cooperative system is possible both in the industrial field (more readily in smaller enterprises) and in the agricultural field, in which Catholics have also advocated and put in practice *collective leasing.*

The Church has always favored the cooperative system as suitable to the principles of social justice, of Christian brotherhood and of human solidarity. Pius XII referred to it in the radio message of September 1, 1944, mentioned above, saying: "Small and medium-sized holdings in agriculture, in arts and trades, in commerce and industry must be guaranteed and fostered; the cooperative unions must assure them the advantages of the big concern."

The same Pontiff, speaking to the owners of small farms, explained this last thought as follows: "You experience the benefits of cooperatives which permit you, whilst yet keeping your small holdings, to enjoy the facilities that are generally associated with big farmer modern labor-saving machines, the improving of soils; the selection of seeds; markets for buying and selling under the best conditions thanks to available capital and to the possibility of storing products and of using them at the right moment." (Discourse to the owners of small farms, May 25, 1956.)

CHAPTER VII

CHRISTIANITY AND CHARITY

Preliminary Notions

1. *Justice* and *Charity* are the two foremost *social* virtues, inasmuch as they dispose our minds to the fulfillment of our duties toward society, so that, after having considered the teachings of Christianity with regard to justice, we are now to treat of charity, called *the queen of virtues.*

Charity is the theological virtue that inclines us to love God for Himself and our neighbor for the love of God. Charity must not only be *affective* (prompted by feeling and sentiment), but also *effective* (productive of effects and of works). Works are the test of charity.

It is not enough to *wish good* to our neighbor; it is also necessary *to do good to him,* according to his needs. Charity has to be converted into *kindness* and *mercy.*

It was this that Our Lord taught by the parable of the Good Samaritan, who "seeing him, was moved with compassion" (affective charity), and forthwith "he went up to him and bound up his wounds," etc. (effective charity). And the parable ends with an admonition to imitate the Good Samaritan who "showed mercy to him." (*Lk.* 10:25-37).

2. Pity, therefore, is charity itself, *insofar as it inclines us to help our neighbor in his spiritual and material needs. It is beneficent* charity.

In fact, man, being composed of body and soul, has *material,* or corporal, and *spiritual* needs. Charity bids us take care of both; hence, the *corporal* and the *spiritual* works of mercy.

57

Pius XII, in *Sertum Laetitiae,* writes these striking words: *"The fundamental point of the social question is this, that the goods created by God for all men should in the same way reach all, justice guiding and charity helping."*

The communists say: "Relief may be necessary today because we are living under a regime of injustice and of exploitation; but when the regime of perfect justice will be restored, as we hope, then it will no longer be necessary to speak of charity and of relief, because there will be no needy persons."

A pretty Utopia! We have seen, in fact, that in virtue of justice we give to others what is due them. Now, even in the best of social regimes, in which the principles of justice would not only be *professed* but *practiced* by everyone (and such a regime is not possible on earth on account of Original Sin), there will always be individuals who, with or without fault on their part (like the poor and the sick), will have needs without rights. So that charity will at times have to fulfill its supplemental role.

God grant (and this should be our wish since it is both feasible and a duty) that the field of this supplemental role of charity may become more and more restricted as the consciousness and the practice of justice become more widespread. However, there will always be people in need and in distress who will have to be helped by charity.

Charity, therefore, fills up the gaps left behind by justice; its arms are longer, its sight keener, and it reaches out to places where justice cannot reach. Charity goes beyond the narrow limits of justice and brings relief where there is no real right, but where there is real need.

The Duty of Charity

Charity is the essence of Christianity and the sum of all the virtues.

Jesus taught the duty of beneficent charity both by His *example* and by His *teaching.*

a) *By His example.*

The life of Christ was one continuous act of kindness: in fact, St. Peter sums it up in this manner: "Jesus went about [upon earth] doing good." (*Acts* 10:38).

To the disciples of St. John who ask Him if He is

the Messias, Jesus, as proof of the fact that He is, points to His good works: "Go and relate to John what you have heard and seen: the blind see, the lame walk, the lepers are cleansed, the deaf hear. . ." (*Matt.* 11:4-5).

Twice He performs the miracle of the *multiplication of loaves* by pronouncing these touching words: "I have compassion on the multitudes, because they continue with me now three days and have nothing to eat and I will not send them away fasting lest they faint on the way." (*Matt.* 15:32-39).

b) *By His teachings.*

Jesus often spoke of the duty of beneficent charity. Suffice it here to recall that at the Last Judgment the sentence that will be pronounced by Him against the reprobates will be this: "Depart from me, accursed ones, into the everlasting fire. . .for I was hungry, and you gave me not to eat: I was thirsty, and you gave me not to drink," etc., and upon being asked for an explanation, He replies: "Amen I say to you, as long as you did not do it to one of these least, neither did you do it to me." (*Matt.* 25:41-45).

What better proof that corporal works of charity constitute a duty when Jesus condemns to eternal suffering those who neglect them?

The Apostles were no less explicit. These quotations will suffice:

St. Paul commands the Christians of Rome to share their goods with their needy brothers: "Loving one another with the charity of brotherhood. . .communicating to the necessities of the saints." (*Rom.* 12:10-13). And writing to the Hebrews, he reminds them of the duty of helping others: "And do not forget to do good, and to impart; for by such sacrifices God's favour is obtained" (namely, His grace). (*Heb.* 13:16).

St. John, on his part, writes these precise words for the hard-hearted: "He that hath the substance of this world, and sees his brother in need, and shall shut up his bowels from him: how does the charity of God abide in him?" (*1 Jn.* 3:17). And shortly before, the same Apostle had taught that: "He that loveth not, abideth in death." (*1 Jn.* 3:14)—and, of course, what he meant is supernatural death.

Comprehension and Extension of Charity

1. The charity commanded by Christ *has the greatest possible comprehension, because there are no limitations to the sacrifices called for by it, including even the sacrifice of life itself.*

The code of Christian charity was written by the Blood of our Saviour; it was sanctioned by His supreme sacrifice. Jesus, in fact, was not content to call us brothers and to teach us brotherly love. He, *the first-born among many brothers* (as St. Paul calls Him), gave His life for them. *"I am the Good Shepherd,"* He said, *"who gives His life for His sheep."*

Thus He taught us that we must give not merely our affection to our brothers, not merely our goods (a sacrifice that can cost us little when the goods are plentiful) but ourselves as well; our strength, our efforts, and our very life when required by the supreme needs of the natural and supernatural life of our neighbors.

The Apostle of Charity, St. John, is very clear on this point, saying, "He hath laid down his life for us: and we ought to lay down our lives for the brethren." (*1 Jn.* 3:16).

To give one's "life for the brethren" is a miracle of the law of Christianity that overthrows the commandments of human selfishness, the supreme law of which is this: to sacrifice everything to one's self, even the life of the brethren.

Such a law of heroic altruism has found and still finds generous champions in our religion. How many missionaries, how many Sisters are dying today in their ministry of charity, in leper colonies, in hospitals, in fields of labor and danger, willing victims for the spiritual and physical welfare of their brethren?

Even soldiers who give their lives in the fields of battle in performance of their duty for the defense of their country, obey this law of altruism.

2. The charity commanded by Christ has also the *greatest possible extension,* because not a single person is excluded.

Here are some enlightening words of Christ: "Do good to them that hate you and pray for them that persecute and calumniate you, that you may be the children of your Father who is in heaven, who maketh his sun to rise upon the good, and bad, and raineth upon the just and the unjust. For if you love them that love you, what reward shall you have? Do not even the publicans this?" (*Matt.* 5:44-46).

The children, like the Father, must love all, do good to all. Universal charity, therefore, is a necessary attribute of universal brotherhood.

This universality of love is another wonderful novelty of the Gospel. The few who in ancient times knew what charity was limited its sphere of action. Cicero said: *"Non nobis solum nati sumus."* "We were not born for ourselves alone." (*De Officiis,* 1:7).

These words are a condemnation of selfishness, but whom besides ourselves must we think about? The pagan philosopher replies: *"Ortus nostri partem patria vindicat, partem parentes, partem amici."* "We owe, therefore, a part of ourselves to our *country,* a part to our *relatives,* a part to our *friends."* And that is all. The vision of the philosopher extends no further.

Jesus Christ has broken these narrow and arbitrary boundaries. Our beneficent charity—He teaches—must embrace all men, precisely because they are all children of one and the same Father, made in the image of One only.

3. But to love our enemies, to love those who have nothing lovable but a great deal that is hateful, to do good to those who have done us harm, is that not an absurd commandment, an unreasonable demand?

That is what some think and say who do not understand, or pay no heed to the motives of Christian love toward one's neighbor. We have said it already: we must love God *for Himself,* but we must love our neighbor not for himself, but for *the love of God:* that is, because God commands it, because in every man there is the image of God, because every man is redeemed by the Blood of Christ, because every Christian is a son of God and our brother. These *claims* to our love are present in *all* men, even in those who *in themselves* are not at all deserving of our love.

Needless to say, our love and our kindness are all the more meritorious in the sight of God the less they are deserved and acknowledged by men.

The Advantages of Beneficent Charity

Charity procures advantages for us both in this life and in the next. The following are the principle ones:

1. CHARITY OPENS THE GATES OF HEAVEN FOR US.

Jesus on the day of the Last Judgment will pronounce these words: "Come, ye blessed of my Father, possess you the kingdom...I was hungry, and you gave me to eat..." (*Matt.* 25:34-36).

2. CHARITY MERITS FOR US THE HELP OF GOD.

Tobias gives his son this advice: "Give alms out of thy substance, and turn not away thy face from any poor person; and it shall come to pass that the face of the Lord shall not be turned from thee." (*Tob.* 4:7). And here, *by alms*, is meant every work of mercy.

3. CHARITY MERITS FOR US THE PARDON OF OUR SINS.

The Archangel Raphael said to Tobias: "For alms deliver from all sin, and from death, and will not suffer the soul to go into darkness." (*Tob.* 4:11).

Our Lord said: "Blessed are the merciful, for they shall obtain mercy." (*Matt.* 5:7).

Wherefore Manzoni is right when he puts these words in the mouth of Lucia: "God forgives many things for an act of mercy." (*The Betrothed,* 21).

The works of mercy—both corporal and spiritual—should therefore hold a prominent place in our Christian life.

Catholic Action is a sort of spiritual work of mercy and is, therefore, a dutiful and meritorious work.

Works of mercy are in themselves very effective means of the apostolate; Pope Pius XII said: "This restless and agitated mankind that is no longer willing to believe in truth, that no longer dares to believe in justice, cannot make up its mind to give up believing in charity." (Discourse of March 13, 1940). Many times by taking care of men's bodies, we heal their souls.

Pius XII, in the discourse above referred to, also stated that: *"The poor in their turn are in many ways benefactors."* For charity always redounds to the benefit of the one that does it. In truth, the best way to do good to ourselves is to do good to others. The benefactor is always the first to benefit.

But for this purpose it is necessary that we avoid every kind of ostentation, mindful of the counsel of Christ: "Therefore, when thou dost an almsdeed sound not a trumpet before thee...let not thy left hand know what thy right hand doth...and thy Father, who seeth in secret, will repay thee." (*Matt.* 6:2-4).

In fine, let us see to it that our charity is *patient* and *kind,* as St. Paul wishes it. In doing charity, let us avoid any air of superiority and of condescension that might humiliate the beneficiary—in other words, let us do *charity charitably.*

CHAPTER VIII

CHRISTIANITY AND AUTHORITY

Preliminary Notions

1. Man is naturally *sociable*, inasmuch as he is destined to live not in isolation, but in society. Not only in domestic society, wherein he is born and reared, but also in *civil society*, which is a natural expansion of the family.

Civil society is necessary because therein only is it possible for man to develop all his faculties and to attain his end. Hence history assures us that man always lived in society. Accordingly, society is not a phenomenon that sprang up by the will of the associates, as some philosophers have fancied, but was ordained by Nature itself, or rather by God, the Creator.

Chief among those philosophers is Jean Jacques Rousseau, who may well be considered the father of liberalism. His book *The Social Contract* exerted a profound influence on the minds of the leaders of the French Revolution of 1789, which overthrew the ancient absolutist regime and inaugurated the popular, or *liberal*, regime.

This philosopher of Geneva taught that at first men lived in a *natural state*, by which he meant the state of absolute liberty, without social ties. Then they got together and formed society through a kind of free agreement (*social contract*). Consequently, civil society is not necessary, but free; it is not an effect of the will of God, but of man.

2. There can be no society of any kind without an *authority*. Thus, just as society comes from God, so likewise does authority.

Authority is justly called the *soul* of society; in fact, just as in the human organism the soul harmonizes the various members and makes them concur toward the common end, which is life, similarly in the social organism, authority is the unifying principle that coordinates the wills of individuals and directs them to one end, which is the *common good*.

Without authority, an aggregation of men may be a crowd, but not a society, either public or private.

Our Lord said: "Every kingdom divided against itself shall be made desolate." (*Matt.* 12:25).

Now, every society without authority is doomed to become divided against itself and hence to fall. Thus history bears witness to another fact: There was never a society without authority. Those who, with Jean Jacques Rousseau, hold that civil society does not come from God, but from man, also hold logically but erroneously that civil authority likewise comes from man. That accounts for their theory of *popular sovereignty*, in the sense that all power is derived not from God, but from the people, truly *sovereign* in the most absolute sense of the world.

The expression *popular sovereignty* can also have this meaning: The people determine the form of government (*popular election*). In this sense, popular sovereignty is admissable, though not necessary. The Church, in fact, has always declared that every form of government—aristocratic or democratic—is legitimate when it is suitable for the achievement of its end, which is *the good of the citizens*.

3. As there are different societies, so there are *different kinds of authority*. The principal ones are the following:

(a) *Religious authority*, that rules the religious

society, which for us Catholics is the Church. This authority resides in the Pope and in the Bishops.

(b) *Civil authority,* that rules civil society and resides in the heads of government (emperors, kings or presidents of republics, and in their ministers and in legislative assemblies.)

(c) *Domestic authority,* which resides in the parents, especially the father, whence it is also called *paternal authority.*

We have already seen in a preceding chapter how Jesus restored paternal authority. We are now going to see how He likewise restored civil authority, which had been corrupted and led astray by paganism.

Civil Authority in the Pagan World

1. Paganism had perverted the idea of the end of civil authority which, according to the intention of God, the Creator, is established *for the good of the citizens, individually and collectively, without distinction.* Whereas, among pagan people, at least at the time of Christ, authority was generally considered as a lordship. The state was free to dispose at will of the life and goods of its subjects, who, instead of *subjects,* might more properly be called *slaves,* and the people *herds.*

The state, among many pagan peoples, had become like the god Moloch of the Phoenicians, to whom parents had to sacrifice their children. The individual was sacrificed to the state, which was all but deified. This system of government was called Caesarism, from the title of the Roman emperor who claimed divine honors.

2. It is evident that *Caesarism* is a *degeneration* of *absolutism,* since it is quite possible to have an absolute government (*the power of one only*) that promotes the welfare of all the subjects according to justice and charity.

Those were the days in which an emperor like Caligula could wish that the people had but a single head, in order that he might amuse himself by cutting it off in one blow. And the poet Horace could sing in a cynical tone: *"Nos numerus sumus, fruges, consumere nati."* "We are mere ciphers, born but to eat up food." The people were considered nothing but ciphers, and it happened not infrequently that they were sacrificed to the whim of a ruler, in a civil war of petty spite, of ambition, or in a vindictive slaughter.

Celebrated in this connection is the slaughter of the Jews ordered by King Assuerus (Artaxerxes) of Persia, in order to humor the whim of his proud and cruel minister, Aman. The latter had become enraged against the Jew, Mardochai, because he refused to adore him, and for revenge asked and obtained from the king the extermination of all of Mardochai's countrymen. (See *Esther, 3, et seq.*).

Also in Christian times not a few rulers continued to be led by the pagan concept of authority cynically championed in the notorious book of Nicolo Machiavelli, *The Prince.*

According to this author a ruler must know how to make good use "of the beast in a man," to play the part of the lion and of the fox, coupling strength with craftiness. Therefore "a ruler, and especially a new ruler, cannot observe all those things whereby men are said to be good, since it is often necessary in order to protect the state to act against the faith, against charity, against humanity, against religion." (Chap. 18).

Jesus Restored Civil Authority

He did this in two ways:
(a) *By teaching its divine origin;*
(b) *By pointing out its end and its limits.*

HE TEACHES THE DIVINE ORIGIN OF AUTHORITY

(a) Jesus taught that *all authority comes from God*—not only religious and paternal authority, but also civil; therefore, authority is something sacred and entitled to the utmost respect.

To Pilate, who reproaches Him for His silence by saying to Him: "Speakest thou not to me? knowest thou
not that I have power to crucify thee, and I have power
to release thee?" Jesus answers solemnly: "Thou
shouldst not have any power against me, unless it were
given thee from above." (*Jn.* 19:10-11). Even the authority of Pilate, like that of every ruler, comes therefore
from above, from God.

Thus Jesus has exalted, ennobled and tempered civil
authority. Little wonder, then, that in Christian times,
kings were anointed after the manner of priests.

(b) If authority comes from God, it is always sacred
and worthy of respect, even when it resides in unworthy persons; subjects, therefore, are bound to obey even
the wicked rulers when their commands are not
manifestly wicked. This was also the teaching of Christ,
who said one day: "The scribes and the Pharisees have
sitten on the chair of Moses. All things therefore whatsoever they shall say to you, observe and do. But according to their works do ye not; for they say, and do not."
(*Matt.* 23:2-3). And when they ask Him if it is lawful
to pay tribute to Caesar (to the Roman emperor, whom
his fellow-countrymen believed to be an unjust oppres-
sor), Jesus replied: "Render to Caesar the things that
are Caesar's, and to God the things that are God's."
(*Matt.* 22:21).

HE POINTS OUT THE END AND THE LIMITS OF AUTHORITY

(a) Jesus teaches that authority is not a lordship
but a *fatherhood,* a *ministry,* a *service.* The subjects do
not exist for the benefit of the former. *The good of the
people* is the end of every civil authority, as well as
its limitation.

Here are the priceless words of Christ, spoken to His
Apostles but applicable to every authority: "You know
that the princes of the Gentiles lord it over them, and
they that are the greater, exercise power upon them.

It shall not be so among you: but whosoever will be the greater among you, let him be your minister: And he that will be first among you, shall be your servant. Even as the Son of man is not come to be ministered unto but to minister, and to give his life a redemption for many." (*Matt.* 20:25-28).

(b) In fact, here too, as elsewhere, Jesus confirms His teaching by His example. Take the touching and suggestive episode of the Last Supper. St. John relates: "Knowing that the Father had given him all things into his hands, and that he came from God, and goeth to God; he riseth from supper, and layeth aside his garments, and having taken a towel, girded himself. After that, he putteth water into a basin, and began to wash the feet of the disciples, and to wipe them with the towel wherewith he was girded." (*Jn.* 13:3-5). And after this action, He explained its significance to them, saying: "For I have given you an example, that as I have done to you, so you do also." (*Jn.* 13:15).

Note the first words of the account: *"[Jesus,] knowing that the Father had given him all things into his hands"*—that is, knowing that He was the *Lord of the Universe* and possessed all power in Heaven and on earth, nevertheless humbles Himself even to the point of performing such a base service, which at that time was done only by *slaves*. Then He says to the future rulers of His Church (and through them to all who hold any power whatever): *"As I have done to you, so you also should do."*

Manzoni tells us that Cardinal Frederick Borromeo had made up his mind at an early date: *"That there is no just superiority of men over men, except in serving them."* That is the true idea of every authority, religious, civil and paternal. The superior must consider himself a *servant* of his subjects, and precisely for this reason—and not through vain ostentation—does the Pope call himself *Servus Servorum Dei:* The Servant of the Servants of God (a title first used by St. Gregory the Great).

Jesus Exalts the Dignity of the Subject

1. By exalting the dignity of the superior (that is, by declaring him vested with an authority that comes from God), Jesus thereby also exalted the dignity of the subject. In fact, the latter, by obeying his superior, in reality does not obey a man like himself, but God Himself. And to obey God is not to demean, but rather to exalt oneself. By that very means Christianity laid the most solid foundation to obedience, which always has God for its final end.

2. Furthermore, Jesus has exalted the individual with respect to authority:

(a) By teaching the truth of *one divine Fatherhood* and, hence, of *universal brotherhood.*

The Christian ruler must look upon his subject not as a *servant,* but as a *brother,* having the same rights before God, their *common Father.* In fact, ruler and subject together say: *"Our Father."*

(b) By teaching *the infinite value of a redeemed soul,* purchased by the Blood of Christ: "Knowing that you were not redeemed with corruptible things as gold or silver,...but with the precious blood of Christ." (*1 Ptr.* 1:18-19).

Jesus, moreover, showed us in a most touching manner the value of a single individual, when He pictured Himself as the Good Shepherd who "has a hundred sheep and one of them go astray and he leaves the other ninety-nine in the mountains and goes in search of the one that has strayed." (*Matt.* 18:12). Even so, Jesus Christ asserts, it is not the will of your Father in Heaven that *"a single one of these little ones should perish."*

The Teachings of the Church

In this matter also, the teachings of Christ found a true echo in the teachings of the Church in every age and among every people.

1. Touching the *divine origin* of authority, we have the explicit testimony of the Apostles. St. Paul teaches the early Christians of imperial Rome: "There is no power but from God;...therefore, he that resisteth the power, resisteth the ordinance of God; and they that resist purchase to themselves damnation...for he is God's minister to thee, for good." (*Rom.* 13:1-4).

St. Peter is no less explicit when he exhorts the faithful as follows: "Be subject to every human creature for God's sake, whether it be to the king as excelling, or to the governors as sent by him for the punishment of evil-doers and for the praise of the good, for so is the will of God." (*1 Ptr.* 2:13-15).

Pope St. Gregory the Great is later to declare: *"Power is given to emperors and kings from Heaven."*

The apologist Tertullian, toward the end of the second century after Christ, wrote: "We venerate in emperors the judgment of God Himself, who placed them at the head of the nations. In them we see the will of God, and therefore we, too, want to safeguard what God has willed."

2. Leo XIII, on the thorny question of the *form of government,* stated categorically: "There is no reason why the Church should not approve of the chief *power being held by one man or by more;* provided, only, it be just, and that it tend to the common good. Wherefore, so long as justice is respected, people are free to choose for themselves the form of government which suits best either their own disposition or the institutions and customs of their ancestors." (Encyclical on Civil Government).

Concerning the *use of authority,* the same Pontiff states: "But in order that justice may be retained in government, it is of the highest importance that those who rule states should understand that *political power was not created for their particular advantage;* and that the administration of the state must be carried on for the benefit of those who have been committed to their care, not for the benefit of those to whom it has been committed." (Encyclical on Civil Government).

3. Developing this idea, Pius XII, in a discourse to a group of members of the Italian Parliament (Dec. 13, 1950) expressed himself as follows: "Superiority is a service; to command is not to act arbitrarily, but in obedience to the external law of truth and justice. You feel, as all must feel, how much strength from God is needed in order to react manfully, in the performance of duty, against selfishness and pride, *always giving preference to the common interests over the private interests of the individual group or party; and to do that solely in the light of justice, of charity and of faith.*"

Concerning the *duties of the State,* Pius XII has taught us: "It is the noble prerogative and function of the State to control, aid and direct the private individual activities of national life so long as to make them concur harmoniously toward *the common good. . ."*

"To consider the State as an end in itself to which everything else must be subordinated and directed cannot but be harmful to the true and lasting prosperity of nations. This can come about either when unlimited power is attributed to the State as the mandatary of the nation, of the people, or even of a social class, or when the State claims such power as absolute master, without any mandate whatever." (Encyclical *Summi Pontificatus*).

From this clear-cut and beneficent Christian doctrine concerning authority, we will draw some practical corollaries:

1. First of all, a deep sense of gratitude to the Divine Redeemer for having conferred upon mankind also this great social blessing— that of having restored authority by making it at once strong and mild, like *fatherhood.*

2. If we occupy some position of authority, whether within or without the family, let us bear in mind our dignity and *responsibility as representatives of God,* to whom we will have to render a strict accounting of the use we have made of the authority we received from Him.

3. All authority ought directly or indirectly to promote the glory of God and the salvation of souls. At least, it must never be a hindrance thereto. It is with such intentions that every Catholic ought to accept and exercise authority.

4. Let us supernaturalize our obedience by looking upon every legitimate authority—not only religious, but civil as well—as a reflection of Divine authority. In that way, our obedience will become at once easier and more meritorious.

CHAPTER IX

CHRISTIANITY AND LIBERTY

Physical Liberty

The word *liberty* is equivalent to *absence of necessity* and has various meanings.

First of all, one should distinguish between *physical* liberty and *moral* liberty:

1. *Physical, or psychological liberty, is the power of man to decide for himself, to will or not to will, to will one thing or another.* This self-determination presupposes an absence of necessity, not merely *external*, but also *internal*.

External necessity, or constraint, derives from a power that lies *outside of man* and compels him to do what he does not want to do. Such is the power that forces an individual to remain shut up in jail, or to ascend the scaffold.

Internal necessity comes instead from an impulse *within man* that forces him to act. Such is the case of a somnambulist, of an insane man, of those who act under the stimulus of an interior power which they cannot control.

From the above we can understand how two cases diametrically opposed to each other may be supposed in man: the case of the external, without any internal necessity (as in the case of the condemned man who walks toward the scaffold because he is obliged to do so against his will), and that of an internal, without any external necessity (as in the case of one who walks in his sleep under the impulse of nervous excitement, without being subject to any external force).

2. The absence of internal necessity is called *free* will, inasmuch as it makes man the arbiter of his own actions.

Free will is an effect of the spirituality of the soul, and is innate in every man. However, *there are internal and external causes that may diminish or destroy free will.* Some such internal causes are: passions, temperaments, habits, ignorance, sleep, insanity. Nervous diseases that produce mental disorders have a more or less pronounced influence upon the will which, as we know, follows the judgment of the mind.

Inasmuch as the extent of the influence of these internal causes is nearly always uncertain, in many cases it is almost impossible for man to determine the exact degree of *responsibility* that attaches to an action, since obviously the *responsibility* of an action is always in proportion to its *freedom.*

Formerly, in judging of the responsibility of human actions, little or no account was taken of the internal causes that take away or diminish the freedom of the will. Today, the tendency is to the other extreme, even to the point of denying freedom itself and thus of every responsibility. Mental diseases, hereditary psychoses, monomania and other morbid conditions have become the stock in trade of criminal lawyers.

3. The existence of free will has often been denied by philosophers and theologians. In ancient times, these persons were called *fatalists* because they held that the will of man was dominated by a higher and mysterious force that is called *fate.* Nowadays, they are called *determinists,* because they claim that every act of the human will is *determined* by an interior irresistible force like insinct in animals.

Modern *determinism* is very largely the result of *materialism.* If man is nothing but matter without a spiritual soul, it is evident that everything in him has to be subject to the inflexible laws of matter, and hence there is no room for freedom.

Fatalism and determinism deprive man of his highest dignity and debase him to the level of the brute, because, as Dante writes:

"The greatest gift God of His largesse made at the creation, and the most conformed to His own excellence, and which He most prizeth, was the will's liberty, wherewith creatures intelligent, both all and alone, were and are endowed." (*Par.* 5:19).

4. There are many *arguments that prove the existence of free will.* We will here mention the two principal ones:

(a) *The testimony of conscience.*

We feel inwardly that it is in our power to act or not to act, to act in one way or in another. We feel, for example, that we have the power to eat or not to eat, to eat much or little, this or that; whereas it does not depend upon us to make a good digestion. Therefore, our very conscience assures us that both *free acts* and *necessary acts* are attributable to us.

A modern philosopher, Antonio Franchi, in his book *Ultimate Critique* makes this shrewd observation: "To *feel free* and to *be free* is the same thing, as it is the same thing to feel happy and to be happy, to feel sad and to be sad, to feel in doubt and to be in doubt. And just as it is impossible to have a feeling of doubt, of sorrow, of joy, without the real state of doubt, or sorrow and of joy, so it is impossible to have a feeling of freedom without the real state of freedom."

(b) *The testimony of mankind.*

Mankind has always praised virtue and blamed vice, rewarded merit and punished guilt. But these words, *praise* and *blame, reward* and *punishment* would have no meaning if a man were not free and hence responsible for his own acts. Were there ever any rewards or punishments established for animals?

Accordingly, the determinists, to be logical, should burn all codes, abolish the courts and close the jails. In fact, some followers of materialistic determinism consistently proposed to convert all jails into sanitariums, considering every criminal either a *patient,* an abnormal being, or a psychopathic case. But this proposal was never taken seriously.

Similarly, *laws, prohibitions, commands, counsels, reproofs,* and *threats* that mankind has always made use of would become practical absurdities if man is not master of his own acts, or acted after the manner of a machine or of an animal.

Moral Freedom

1. *Moral freedom* is entirely different from physical freedom, though having its roots in the latter. It consists in the *power of doing everything that is not forbidden by a just law.*

Moral freedom is therefore a right, the object of which is the *good.* No one has a right to do evil. Therefore, the power of doing evil is a defect and does not belong to the essence of freedom, just as tendency to sickness does not belong to the essence of health. Therefore, as Leo XIII teaches us in his Encyclical *Libertas* on Human Freedom: "Thus it is that the infinitely perfect God, although supremely free, because of the supremacy of His intellect and of His essential goodness, nevertheless cannot choose evil; neither can the angels and the saints who enjoy the beatific vision. St. Augustine and others urged most admirably against the Pelagians that if the possibility of deflection from good belonged to the essence or perfection of liberty, then God, Jesus Christ, and the angels and saints, who have not this power, would have no liberty at all, or would have less liberty than man has in his state of pilgrimage and imperfection."

Consequently, public authorities, while allowing full liberty to goodness, cannot equate liberty to evil and to error. That would not be true liberty, but *license.*

Social order and peace are based upon a proper balance between authority and liberty. It cannot be denied that this balance is difficult of achievement, for both authority and liberty are easily abused. Thus history bears witness that peoples frequently pass all of a sudden from an excess of authority (authoritarianism) to an excess of liberty (libertarianism).

2. There are *different kinds of moral freedom,* according to the objects upon which it is exercised. Thus we have *religious, civil, economic, professional, scientific* freedom, and so on.

The liberals, by posing as the champions of all liberties, have proclaimed the *liberty of thought,* of *conscience* and of *religion* in opposition to the Church that prescribes dogmas to be believed and religious acts to be performed. What are we to think of such liberties?

If, by these words, the liberals mean that religion cannot be imposed by force, they are stating the truth, but they are not stating anything that has not already been proclaimed by the Church. Religion is a free homage to God; and no one can be forced to believe or to profess that which he does not believe.

Alcuin in his famous letter to Emperor Charlemagne who, with unenlightened zeal, was seeking to convert the Saxons to Christianity with the sword rather than with the word, admonished him: "Remember that the faith, as St. Augustine defines it, is an *act of the will* and not of violence. Man may be drawn to faith, but he cannot be forced into it. You may drive people to baptism, but you cannot make them take one step forward toward religion. Therefore, those who evangelize the pagans must use words of peace with the people, because Our Lord knows the hearts that He wants, and enlightens them so that they may understand." Leo XIII referred to this teaching in his Encyclical *Immortale Dei:* "It is the absolute will of the Church that no one be forced to embrace the Catholic Faith because, as St. Augustine wisely observes, *man cannot believe except by his own free will."*

3. But the liberals by those words mean to affirm that *"each one is free to profess the religion that pleases him and even profess none at all,"* as Leo XIII states in his Encyclical *Libertas;* they mean liberty to think and to do whatever one wishes concerning God; they mean, in a word, *religious indifferentism.*

Now this unlimited freedom in religious matters would be lawful only in the event that it were not possible to know the true God and the true religion. But such is not the case, because the existence of God and Christian revelation are truths that can be proved and have been proved by human reason.

Therefore, to these statements, so common in our days: "Man is free to think as he pleases. . .he is free to profess the religion that he likes best"—and other similar statements, we answer as follows: "He is free *physically,* but not *morally."* In the same way, a son is free to honor or to dishonor his father.

Christ and Freedom

1. The dogma of the *physical freedom* of man is clearly set forth in the Old Testament.

We read in *Genesis* that God, in creating man, uttered these significant words, which are not employed for any other creature: "Let us make man to our image and likeness." (*Gen.* 1:26). Now, this *likeness* (not *equality*) is derived from the fact that man has a spiritual and immortal soul and a free will. *Spirituality, immortality, freedom,* are attributes of God.

In *Ecclesiasticus* we read these words: "God made man from the beginning and left him in the hand of his own counsel. . .Before man is life and death, good and evil; that which he shall choose shall be given to him." (*Ecclus.* 15:14-18).

The New Testament takes for granted the freedom of the will. The whole preaching of Christ would be an absurd labor, all His precepts and counsels would be but empty words, if man were forced to act automatically or instinctively. The whole plan of the Gospel would have no reason for existence, because fallen man would not be capable of redemption, and the punishment of *eternal fire,* with which Jesus threatened the reprobates (*Matt.* 25:41) would be an unheard-of cruelty. For whoever is not free is not responsible for what he does and deserves neither reward nor punishment.

2. Holy Writ also also proclaims and defends *moral liberty.*

Already in the Old Testament, God is pictured as the Deliverer from the many ills that man has brought upon man. The Psalmist hails Him thus: "My refuge, my support, and my deliverer." (*Ps.* 143:2).

But the true *Deliverer,* the Restorer of every legitimate freedom, is the *God-man.* Jesus championed the liberty of man, as such, even before the liberty of the citizen, the worker, etc., for as we have seen, *slavery* was the social condition of the great majority of men.

And this work of social redemption He accomplished not with violent means, not by demagogic expedients, but by the peaceful preaching of lofty moral principles which, like grains of yeast, penetrated into the great mass of humanity and gradually transformed it.

The first principle is that of the *substantial equality* of all men, *made to the image and likeness of One only,* that is of God, the Creator, and redeemed by the same Blood of Christ, who commanded that the message of redemption be brought to men of all races and of all nations: "Preach the gospel to every creature." (*Mk.* 16:15).

Another principle is that of the *brotherhood of man,* which the Redeemer proclaimed in the plainest way when, before a group of men of different social classes, He said: "All you are brethren." (*Matt.* 23:8).

More sublime, still, and more decisive is the principle of *adoption as sons of God,* granted to all the baptized: "Who are born not of blood, nor of the will of the flesh, nor of the will of man, but of God." (*Jn.* 1:13). That means that the loftiest nobility has been granted even to those who occupy the lowest spheres in the social order.

From all these evangelical principles, there springs forth as a practical corollary: the *moral* freedom of every man. And, in truth, to equal subjects belong equal rights. Neither can a brother fetter a brother, nor a son of God become a slave of man.

Hence it appears that the famous and much-abused threefold label of the French Revolution—*equality, fraternity, liberty*—in its genuine meaning is but a radiatión of the teaching of the Gospel.

Ernest Renan himself, who wrote of the Gospels in a sacrilegious manner, was compelled to confess in his *Marcus Aurelius* that: "the abolition of slavery dates from the day in which the slave—that being whom the ancients conceived as devoid of moral stature—became the moral equal of his master." And it was the Gospel that proclaimed him such an equal.

The Church and Freedom

1. The Church, walking in the footsteps of Christ, was at all times the champion and the protector of every legitimate liberty and the enemy of every tyranny.

First of all, the Church championed the *physical liberty* of man and thus defended the crown of this king of creation.

She condemned the theories of those heretics—like Luther, Calvin and Jansen—who held that Original Sin had destroyed free will, and in our days it condemned the nefarious doctrines of determinism and materialism.

Leo XIII, in his Encyclical *Libertas,* says: "Like the simplicity, sprirituality, and immortality of the soul, so likewise its liberty; no one has affirmed in stronger terms or championed them more consistently than the Church that teaches them at all times, and upholds them as a dogma."

2. The Church, moreover, in the same way that she defended rights of authority against anarchistic theories, so she upheld the rights of moral freedom against the claims and the violence of oppressors. The Church of Christ, from its inception, not the French Revolution of 1789, was the first to proclaim the *rights of man.*

St. Paul, writing to the Christians of Ephesus, exhorts them: "And you, masters, do the same things to them [the slaves], forbearing threatenings, knowing that the Lord both of them and you is in heaven; and there is no respect of persons with him." (*Eph.* 6:9). And to the Christians of Galatia he clearly states: "There is neither Jew nor Greek; there is neither bond nor free: there is neither male nor female. For you are all one in Christ Jesus." (*Gal.* 3:28).

That means that before God there is no difference, either of *nationality* or of *social condition,* or of sex, contrary to what was then held among pagan peoples and among the Jews themselves.

These words of the Apostle of the Gentiles—which have since been reiterated unceasingly by the rulers of the Church—are clear condemnation of *slavery,* which among Christians soon ceased to exist in their minds, if not in their outward practices. The Christian master was bound to see a brother in his slave.

3. But the most effective teachings of the Church were, as always, her actions. In the internal life of the Church, slavery was soon abolished by means of the equal treatment that was accorded to free men and slaves. All, without distinction, were admitted to the same Sacraments, to the same honors, to the same spiritual favors. The words of St. Paul, *"There is no difference between a slave and a freeman,"* immediately became a reality in the liturgical life of the Church.

Some do not give credit to Christianity for this immense social benefit—to wit, the *abolition of slavery*—for the reason that there is no clear condemnation of this social plague in the Gospel, nor has the Church ever launched a campaign against it.

Now here we must make ourselves clear. It is true that the Church, like Christ, never preached a crusade against slavery and that neither has she ever urged the slaves to rebel. By so doing she would have put the world in turmoil. At that time slavery, as we have seen, was one of the props of social life. Therefore, the sudden suppression of slavery would not only have caused confusion, but also damage to everybody and to everything. The Church preferred, as always, *evolution* to *revolution,* by means of a slow, peaceful work of education, without violence and without upheavals.

The reform had to start in souls, in order to be translated little by little into actions and into laws. Experience, in fact, teaches that lasting and beneficial reforms spring from within man and cannot be imposed by force from without. Hence the proverb: *"Whatever is forced does not last."* The Church, therefore, following the example of Christ, achieved this great work of transformation, above all, by her teachings, proclaiming a sound doctrine of equality.

4. The Church has made the highest proclamation of the highest liberty—religious liberty—through the martyrdom of countless sons of hers. Martyrdom is the declaration of the most sacred rights of man, written in blood. The purple army of Christian martyrs is an heroic defense of freedom.

Dante, in the *Divine Comedy,* puts in the mouth of Virgil the famous words: "He seeketh liberty, which is so dear, as knoweth he who life for her refuseth." (*Purg.* II: i 71-72).

No one is better entitled to pronounce these words than the martyr of Christ, who has surrendered his life in order to save the dearest of all liberties, the liberty to serve the True God.

Thus Pius XII teaches us to distinguish between *liberty* and *license,* which is liberty without restraint and without limitations. "True liberty," he writes, "that which truly deserves this name and which constitutes the happiness of peoples, has nothing in common with license, with brazenness. True liberty is just the contrary of that. It is that which guarantees the profession and the practice of what is true and of what is just under the guidance of the divine commandments within the sphere of public welfare. It has therefore need of just limitations." (Message to the Swiss People: Sept. 21, 1946).

Thus, Leo XIII in his Encyclical *Libertas* condemns *freedom of worship,* of *speech,* of the *press,* of *teaching* and of *conscience* as understood by liberalism, which would grant the same rights to good and evil, to truth and error.

However, while *freedom of evil is always unlawful, the toleration of evil* may at times be advisable. On this point Leo XIII teaches: "Without granting any rights except to truth and honesty, the Church, in order to avoid a greater evil, or to achieve or preserve a greater good, does not forbid public authority to tolerate certain things that are at variance with truth and justice."

Pius XII in his Encyclical *Summi Pontificatus* condemns an opposite error, to wit: *Statism,* which *accords unrestricted power to the State,* to the prejudice of the liberty of the individual and of the family, pointing out "that man and the family are by nature prior to the State and that the Creator endowed both with certain powers and rights and assigned to each a mission answering to positive natural exigencies."

CHAPTER X

CHRISTIANITY AND THE LAW

General Notions

1. Moral liberty, as we have seen, finds its limitations in law.

The aspects of law are manifold. In general: by law is meant *a constant manner of being and of acting*.

This manner of acting is *either necessary or free*, according to the nature of different beings.

Thus we have the first division of law into *physical* and *moral*.

Physical law is the manner of acting of beings devoid of reason. Their actions are necessary. The following are examples of physical laws: Bodies fall toward the center of the earth; fire burns; water wets.

The *moral law* regulates, instead, the actions of rational and hence free beings, like men. Moral laws, for example, are those that oblige man to honor God, to respect his parents, to speak the truth, etc.

The moral law may be defined as a *norm of human conduct promulgated by a legitimate authority for the common good*.

Frequently, instead of *moral law* we simply use the word morals. Hence we speak of *Christian morals* to indicate Christian laws as a whole; of *pagan morals*, to signify the rules of paganism as a whole, etc.

Instead of *morals*, we also use the word *ethics*.

2. Moral law is divided into *natural* and *positive*. Natural law is so called because it is *impressed on*

nature and made known by the very nature of man, that is to say, by his reason.

The author of natural law is, therefore, the author of human nature Himself, to wit, God. Natural law is universal, that is, it is bonding on all men: It is *equal* for all and is *immutable.*

As such it is *naturally* known by all men without the need of revelation, divine or human; for, as has been said, it is the light of *reason* itself, the voice of *conscience* which tells us what is good (and consequently to be done) and what is evil (and consequently to be avoided).

All men—even the savage in the Stone Age, even a seven-year-old child—have notions, however vague, of good and evil, of what is right and what is wrong. They feel, for instance, that it is unlawful to steal, to kill, to lie, and that it is right to obey their superiors, to keep their word, to pay their debts, etc.

The whole of these *commands of conscience* forms in effect the natural law.

St. Paul affirms in his letter to the Romans that the pagans, who had no written law (as had the Jews), "are a law unto themselves. They show the work of the law written in their hearts." (*Rom.* 2:14-15). And he adds that in the Last Judgment they will be judged by God, according to this natural law which is prior to all written law and is known by all men.

3. *Positive law* is not made known by natural reason, but by an act of the legislator who promulgates it. It is divided into *divine* and *human,* according to whether the legislator is God or man.

(a) *Divine positive law* can only be known through revelation.

We have the *Old Law* (Old Testament) that was revealed before Christ and the *New Law* (New Testament), which is also called Christian or evangelical, because it was revealed by Christ, the substance of which is contained in the Gospels and other books of the New Testament:

(b) *Human positive law* is either *ecclesiastical* or *civil,* according as it comes from religious or civil authority.

Relationship Between Human Law and Natural Law

Between human law and natural law there are necessary relations.

1. First of all human law has its *foundation,* its *source* and its *binding force* in the natural law. Indeed, since men are *by nature* equal, no man by himself has any authority over another man. Therefore, no man has the power to oblige, that is, to *bind in conscience,* his equal. But the natural law—the expression of the will of God—calls for a human authority in every society (as we have seen in Chapter VIII), and to this authority it confers the power to command and to bind.

For this reason, in the Book of Proverbs, divine Wisdom affirms: "By me, kings reign, and lawgivers decree just things; by me, princes rule and the mighty decree justice." (*Prov.* 8:15-16).

2. Human law has *its sanction and its limitations* in the natural law. That means that the lawgiver must always be guided by and conform to the rules of the natural law, nor may he decree anything contrary to it. When a human law contradicts the natural and divine law, *"it is not a true law"*—declares Thomas Aquinas—*"but a corruption of law."*

In such a case, the law is obviously *not binding in conscience.* In fact, the binding force of a law is wholly derived from God. Now how can God oblige one to do something contrary to His will? He would be contradicting Himself.

3. From this we are able to understand the supreme *importance of the natural law,* without which the whole

structure of human legislation would collapse.

The existence of natural law is so evident, and its function so necessary, that nearly all the ancient pagan philosophers—especially the highest like Plato, Aristotle and Cicero—recognized it and proclaimed its sovereign rights. Cicero called it *"the true and chief law, and right reason of the Supreme Jove."*

In spite of this, many modern philosophers (naturalists, positivists, idealists), by denying God as a transcendent Being consequently deny the natural law and acknowledge only human law. Some, following the theories of the idealist, George Hegel, have deified the State, making it the supreme and only source of every law and every right and duty.

It is evident, for the right reasons already mentioned, that political authority is not thereby exalted, but debased, since it is stripped of its rightful claim to command; and at the same time, the laws are emptied of all their intrinsic efficacy.

These ideas about law—dictated by natural reason itself—are confirmed by the teachings of Christ and of the Church.

The Teachings of Christ

1. Jesus Christ could not have proclaimed the binding force of human laws with greater effect than by submitting Himself to them. And that is what He did with exemplary exactness, although He was not bound to do so because He, as God, was superior to all law. As a perfect citizen He observed the just laws of His country, both ecclesiastical and civil.

As a child He submitted to the prescribed ceremony of circumcision, and later to that of the Presentation in the Temple. When He was twelve years old, "a child of the law," He went with His parents to Jerusalem for the Passover, according to another requirement of the Jewish code.

2. At the beginning of His public life, some were of the opinion that the Messias, by inaugurating a new

kingdom, wanted to do away with the heavy burden of Mosaic law; but He disabused them by stating: "Do not think that I have come to destroy the law or the prophets. I am not come to destroy, but to fulfill" (*Matt.* 5:17), that is to say, to bring the law to perfection.

In fact, He showed Himself a faithful observer of decrees and rites according to law. He cured ten lepers, but since the Mosaic law required that the leper when healed should betake himself to the priests with gifts according to the rite of purification (*Lev.* 14), He said to them: "Go, show yourselves to the priests." (*Lk.* 17:14).

Jesus also observed the *laws of taxation.* Among the Jews, all men who reached twenty years of age had to pay an annual tribute of *two drachmas* for the temple of Jerusalem. The Son of God, too, paid this tribute; and for that purpose He performed a miracle.

This charming episode took place at Capharnaum and is related to us in these words:

"And when they had come to Capharnaum those who were collecting the didrachma came to Peter, and said, 'Doth not your master pay the didrachmas?' He said: Yes. And when he was come into the house, Jesus prevented him, saying: What is thy opinion, Simon? The kings of the earth, of whom do they receive tribute or custom? of their own children, or of strangers? And he said: Of strangers. Jesus said to him: Then the children are free. But that we may not scandalize them, go to the sea, and cast in a hook: and that fish which shall first come up, take: and when thou hast opened its mouth, thou shalt find a stater: take that, and give it to them for me and thee." (*Matt.* 17:23-26).

Jesus, the *Son of God,* was exempt from paying tribute for the *support of religion.* Nevertheless, He paid it! What an example of obedience to law!

When He was asked "if it is lawful to pay tribute to Caesar" (who was considered an usurper by His countrymen), He simply replied: "Render therefore to Caesar the things that are Caesar's." (*Matt.* 22:21); that is to say, give him the coin of the tribute because it belongs to him.

3. He preached obedience even to *wicked lawgivers,* like the scribes and Pharisees, by saying: "The scribes and the Pharisees have sitten on the chair of Moses. All things, therefore, whatsoever they shall say to you, observe and do. But according to their works do ye not; for they say, and do not." (*Matt.* 23:2-3).

But Jesus refused obedience to *wicked laws,* to unjust rules, to arbitrary requirements with which the Pharisees had padded the Mosaic law (like the requirements concerning the various ablutions, and the Sabbath rest that had become an unbearable and unreasonable burden). He publicly complained that the Pharisees *"bind heavy and insupportable burdens, and lay them on men's shoulders."* (*Matt.* 23:4). And He rebuked them severely, saying: *"Well do you make void the commandment of God that you may keep your own tradition."* (*Mk.* 7:9).

Teachings of the Church

1. The Apostles, the immediate heirs of the thought of Christ, preached compliance with all just laws, even when made by pagan lawgivers or by persecutors of the Church. St. Paul made this recommendation to the Christians of Rome: "Wherefore be subject of necessity [to civilian authorities] not only for wrath, but also for conscience' sake. For therefore also you pay tribute. For they [the lawgivers] are the ministers of God, serving unto this purpose. Render therefore to all men their dues. Tribute, to whom tribute is due; custom, to whom custom: fear, to whom fear: honour, to whom honour." (*Rom.* 13:5-7).

Hence it follows that the Christian must observe the law, not only through *fear* of punishment but also as a duty binding in *conscience,* that is to say, out of regard for God Himself, since lawgivers are *ministers of God,* namely instruments of His will insofar as they promulgate just laws.

St. Paul's conduct was in keeping with his teachings. Before the tribunal of Festus, he was able to defend himself with these words which no one could gainsay: *"Neither against the law of the Jews nor against the temple nor against Caesar have I offended in any thing."* (*Acts* 25:8).

Tertullian in his *Apologetic* shows that Christians were an asset to the Roman Empire also because they paid their taxes, whereas the pagans defrauded the government. He writes: "You should be thankful to the Christians, who pay their taxes with exactness because it is forbidden them to defraud anyone."

2. The Pontiffs have repeatedly taught the same doctrine, adding that in one case only is a Christian exempt from the duty of obedience: when there is a question of a law that is clearly unjust and, therefore, contrary to the will of God. Here are the explicit words of Leo XIII: "One reason only can men have for not obeying, namely if something is required of them that is clearly inconsistent with natural and divine law, for it is equally wrong either to command or to do anything in which the law of nature or the will of God is violated. If it should happen, therefore, that one finds himself obligated to choose between these two things, that is to say, to despise the commandments of God or those of rulers, he must obey Jesus Christ, who commanded to render *'to Caesar the things that are Caesar's and to God the things that are God's';* and so following the example of the Apostles one must courageously reply: *'We must obey God rather than man.'* (*Acts* 5:29). Nor can those who behave in such manner be accused of being guilty of disobedience, for if the will of the rulers is repugnant to the will and the laws of God, they themselves exceed the limits of their power and thwart justice; nor can their authority avail in such case, for authority is null when there is no justice." (Encyclical *Diuturnum*).

3. Recent Pontiffs have repeatedly condemned the

error of those who deny the natural law. Pius XII in his Encyclical *Summi Pontificatus* says: "Once the authority of God and the sway of His Law is denied in this way, the civil authority as an inevitable result tends to attribute to itself that absolute autonomy which belongs exclusively to the Supreme Maker. It puts itself in the place of the Almighty and *elevates the State or group into the last end of life, the supreme criterion of the moral and juridical order,* thereby forbidding every appeal to the principles of natural reason and of the Christian conscience."

And further on, the same Pontiff calls our attention to certain injuries caused by this denial of the natural law in the following words: "Where the dependence of human right upon divine right is denied, where appeal is made only to some insecure idea of a merely human authority, and an autonomy is claimed which rests only upon a utilitarian morality, there human law itself *justly forfeits in its more weighty application* the moral force which is the essential condition for its acknowledgment and also for its demand of sacrifice."

Christianity, therefore, while tempering scepters, gives strength to laws. That is another notable social blessing.

On our part we should endeavor to obey human laws for *conscience's* sake, as St. Paul exhorts us to do. We will thus acquire merits not only with men who do not always recognize them, but also with God, who always recognizes them and rewards them for all eternity.

CHAPTER XI

CHRISTIANITY AND LOVE OF COUNTRY

Preliminary Notions

1. The word *patria* is derived from *pater* (father) and is synonymous with "fatherland." It is the place where we were born. As a synonym for country, one may also employ the word *nation,* which has more or less the same meaning, being derived from the word *nascere* (to be born).

Love of country is *natural;* that is, it springs spotaneously in the heart of man. Just as nature itself makes flowers bloom in the fields, so likewise it makes "the love of our native land spring up in our heart." (*Inf.* 14:1).

How can we help loving the land that we were born and grew up in; the land that left its stamp upon our bodies, upon our minds and even upon our voice; the land that harbors our father's home, in which we were reared, the temple where we became sons of God, and a hundred other things that are indelibly engraved in our imagination and in our hearts?

2. But one's country is not merely a place and an aggregate of endearing things, it is also, above all, the community of the people who were born in the land of our birth and who avail themselves of the things that we also avail ourselves of; in a word, it is the whole of our fellow citizens.

This is the loftiest and the truest idea of country. It is also an eminently *Christian* idea. Love of country thus understood is nothing but a manifestation of love of neighbor. It is a natural extension of our love toward our father; an expansion of our love for our family.

3. Love of country, understood in this latter sense too, is a natural sentiment; it was felt even by pagans, who were fond of this motto: *"pro aris et focis"* (for our altars and our fires)—that is, for religion and for country.

But, as happens with all pagan virtues, this too was defiled by spurious elements. Very often it was a case of exaggerated love and pride, that not only disregarded the rights of mankind, but did violence to them. Thus, for the Greeks, every foreigner was a *barbarian,* and for the Romans, an *enemy.*

Even the people of Israel, although taught by God, had an exaggerated idea of country that was often in conflict with their duties toward mankind.

Christianity purified and elevated this virtue also by reconciling it with all of man's duties.

We will see that love of country is a *natural* and a *Christian* duty, founded on the *example of Christ and of the Apostles,* as well as on the *teachings of the Church.* Finally, we will show how *we ought to love our country.*

A Natural and Christian Duty

1. Love of country was a *natural duty* before becoming a Christian duty. The Holy Spirit dictated this sentence: *"Every beast loveth its like: so also every man him that is nearest to himself."* (*Ecclus.* 13:19). These words contain a fundamental law of nature: Love has its motive and its foundation in likeness—the greater and deeper are the likenesses, the keener is the love.

Now, who are our fellow countrymen if not neighbors with whom we have the most in common? In fact, besides having their nature, origin and destiny in common with us, like all men, they have other particular elements of likeness, such as language, culture, traditions, customs, tastes, social relations, common moral and even physical traits.

Love of country, therefore, has its foundations in nature. Patriotism is an inborn sentiment; hence, it is willed and enjoined by the Creator.

From this we can see how senseless is this statement of the *Communist Manifesto*, drawn up by Karl Marx and Frederick Engels: "Workingmen have no fatherland."

And senseless, too, is this other statement which Manzoni puts in the mouth of Don Abbondio: "Fatherland is where one is well off."

2. Love of country is also *a duty of gratefulness for the benefits* that the citizen has received from the people and from the country in which he was born and reared.

St. Thomas Aquinas says on this point: "After God, man is chiefly indebted to his parents and to his country, and, therefore, just as religion must render worship to God, so, to a lesser degree, piety must pay honor to parents and to country."

3. Love of country is a *Christian duty*, inasmuch as it was not only practiced, but preached by Christ who made love of neighbor the characteristic and the novelty of His message: "This is my commandment: that you love one another.". . . (*Jn.* 15:12). "A new commandment I give you; that you love one another." (*Jn.* 13:34). Now, *our closest neighbors*, after those that come in contact with us within the walls of our homes, are those that we come in contact with as soon as we cross the threshold of our homes, within the boundaries of our country.

Indeed, Jesus, the second Adam, came to save *all* the descendants of the first Adam and, therefore, just as He teaches the brotherhood of all men, so likewise He enjoins *universal* love. Because of this universality, some accuse the Gospel of obstructing love of country, but that is a gross error, when it is not a polemical trick. Indeed, love of neighbor, while universal *in extension*, cannot be equally so in *comprehension.*

With regard to its comprehension, there are different degrees of love depending upon greater or lesser likeness, in the sense already explained. Therefore, the prime center of love of neighbor is the family, where the traits of resemblance are more numerous and more marked; from the family it spreads to the country, and from there, to the whole of mankind.

Love of country may be compared to the flame in the fireplace, that warms all who are gathered within the same room, yet reserving however a more intense heat for those who are closest. Hence, we love our countrymen more than foreigners, and the members of our family more than our countrymen. And just as love of home is in harmony with love of country, so love of country is consistent with love of mankind.

The Example of Christ and the Apostles

1. Jesus taught us the duty to love our country, first of all by His conduct. He showed, in fact, a special love for His country.

His preaching was reserved for the children of Israel, and to the Canaanite woman He answers: "I was not sent except to the sheep that are lost of the house of Israel." (*Matt.* 15:24).

The people were aware of this predilection of Jesus for His country, so much so that at Capharnaum, the elders of the Jews, while pleading with Him to come to save the servant of the centurion, said to Him: "He is worthy that thou shouldest do this for him, for he loveth our nation and he has built us a synagogue." (*Lk.* 7:5-6).

Jerusalem, the capital of His people, rejected His kindness. He was saddened by it, and one day He uttered these words full of motherly tenderness: "Jerusalem, Jerusalem...how often would I have gathered thy children together, as a hen gathers her young under her wings, but thou wouldst not!" (*Matt.* 23:37).

A few days before His death, while approaching Jerusalem and looking down upon it from a height, He thought of the terrible lot that awaited that magnificent city, of which there would not be left a stone upon a stone, and tearfully He offered these words, burning with love and desire: "If thou also hadst known, and that in this thy day, the things that are to thy peace; but now they are hidden from thy eyes." (*Lk.* 19:42).

How Jesus loved His country!

2. The *Apostles*, too, brought up in the school of Christ, gave undoubted proof of this love.

They were sent by the Redeemer to teach all nations; but their first concern was for their countrymen within the boundaries of their country, and when, after crossing these boundaries, they entered into a strange city to preach the new message, their first word was always for the Jews that dwelt there.

St. Paul, too, the *Apostle of the Gentiles*, the zealous champion of the universality of Christianity, who had made himself *all things to all men,* when he set foot in a city the first thing he did was to enter the synagogue and to preach the Gospel to his countrymen. He confessed that when he lived among the Jews— who were very much attached to their ceremonies and their customs—*he became a Jew himself* (that is, he lived like them) *that he might gain them to Christ.* (*1 Cor.* 9:20). He went so far as to say that he longed to be excommunicated (if that were possible and necessary) provided that he could save those who were bound to him by ties of blood. "For I wished myself to be an anathema from Christ, for my brethren, who are my kinsmen according to the flesh." (*Rom.* 9:3). Thus did St. Paul hearken to the voice of blood.

The Teachings of the Church

1. The Church of Christ has always taught the duty of loving one's country in preference to others. She has

stressed this duty even during tragic hours, when Christians were subjected to bloody persecutions by public authorities. Tertullian gives us conclusive proof in his *Apologetic*, written at a time when Christians were being persecuted by the Roman emperors as enemies of their country. Here are his exact words: "With eyes lifted up to Heaven, with arms outstretched, incapable of harm, with head uncovered because we are unashamed, we heartily invoke long life for all our emperors, security for the empire, tranquility for families, a powerful army, a faithful servant, a peaceful world and all that men and emperors hope for." (Chapter 30).

2. The Roman Pontiffs have also stressed this duty, pointing out how, in practice, it can and should be fulfilled. Leo XIII said in this regard: "The supernatural love for the Church and the natural love of country are two loves that have their origin in the same eternal principle, since the same God is the author of the one and of the other." (Encyclical *Sapientiae Christianae*).

Pius XII has defended the teaching of the Church in these exact words: "Nor need there be any fear lest the consciousness of universal brotherhood, fostered by the teaching of Christianity, and the spirit which it inspires, be in contrast with love of the traditions or the glories of one's fatherland, or impede the progress of prosperity or legitimate interests. For that same Christianity teaches *that in the exercise of charity we must follow a God-given order, yielding the place of honor in our affections and good works to those who are bound to us by special ties.*" (Encyclical *Summi Pontificatus*).

3. The Church of Christ, however, while teaching and enjoining love of country, has at the same time endeavored to keep it within just bounds by harmonizing it with other loves, according to the dictates of reason and of faith.

Christianity is the religion of harmonies. It teaches *true* love of country, which lies midway between two erroneous extremes: between exaggerated *nationalism,* which ignores the rights of humanity, and *internationalism,* which denies country.

Pius XI, in his Encyclical *Ubi Arcano Dei,* says: "Patriotism, the stimulus of so many virtues and of so many noble acts of heroism, when kept within the bounds of the laws of Christ, becomes merely an occasion, an added incentive to grave injustice when true love of country is debased to the condition of *extreme nationalism* when we forget that all men are our brothers and members of the same human family, that other nations have an equal right with us both to life and to prosperity."

And Pius XII has said that Catholics "just as they should be second to none in their love of country and therefore should love the land of their ancestors with affection and promote its true prosperity, so likewise, guided by Christian precepts, let them embrace the whole human family in the divine love of Jesus Christ, whatever may be the race, whatever may be the people by which it is made up." (Letter to the President of Italian Catholic Action Youth.)

4. A Christian, besides belonging to civil society, belongs also to religious society, namely the Church. Hence the two loves must be in harmony with each other. The following is a teaching of Leo XIII on this point:

> "Now if the natural law commands us to love with devotion and to defend the country in which we were born so that every good citizen does not hesitate to face death for his native land, very much more is the urgent need of Christians to be ever quickened by like feelings toward the Church. For the

Church is the holy city of the living God, born
of God Himself and by Him built and established. Upon this earth indeed she accom-
plishes her pilgrimage, but by instructing and
guiding men she summons them to eternal
happiness. *We are bound then to love dearly
the country whence we have received the means
of enjoyment this mortal life affords, but we
have a much more urgent obligation to love,
with ardent love, the Church to which we owe
the life of the soul, a life that will endure for-
ever. For fitting it is to prefer the good of the
soul to the well-being of the body, inasmuch
as duties toward God are of a far more hal-
lowed character than those toward men."*
(Encyclical *Sapientiae Christianae*).

How One's Country Is to Be Loved

1. Love of country, like love of neighbor generally,
should be not only *affective,* but also *effective.*

When is that the case?

When legitimate authority is respected and all just
laws observed; when citizens are men of integrity,
honest and industrious; when the duties of justice and
charity are fulfilled; when all sacrifices that the country justly calls for are accomplished.

Now who does not see that these are virtues taught
and fostered by the religion of Christ?

2. While on the one hand Christianity teaches and
enjoins such love, on the other she offers the means
to make it effective; these are the principles of the Gospel and the help of divine grace.

Love of country, therefore, cannot be divorced from
respect for religion. Whoever opposes harms his country.

All history affirms the prophet's sentence: *"Happy
is that people whose God is the Lord."* (*Ps.* 143:15).

Pius XII gave utterance to this remarkable sentence,

which history confirms. "He serves his country best who serves his God with greater faith." (Message to the President of the United States: August 26, 1946.)

Silvio Pellico—a great Italian patriot and a great believer—wrote these famous words: "If anyone despises religion, the sanctity of marriage, decency, righteousness and shouts 'my country, my country,' do not believe him. He is a hypocrite of patriotism. He is the poorest kind of a citizen." (*The Duties of Men.*)

More than once, Pius XI gave this admonition to the members of Catholic Action: *"You should be the best citizens."* The admonition was, is and will be observed always and everywhere. Moreover, by the very fact that Catholic Action works for the spread of the Kingdom of Christ it helps to make the whole country a nation of *good citizens,* and that means to make the country truly great. Thus Catholic Action is a peaceful army fighting *pro aris et focis,* for our altars and our homes.

CHAPTER XII

CHRISTIANITY AND PEACE

General Notions

St. Thomas Aquinas, in his *Summa Theologica,* defined peace as: *"The tranquillity of order, particularly in the will."*

Peace is tranquillity, to wit: the absence of disturbances, disorders, and of strife; and such tranquillity rests upon order, which comes from the regular convergence of means to an end, by virtue of which everything finds itself in its proper place.

True order is first of all that *internal* and *moral* order that is found in wills before it is found in things, in wills guided by justice, which is respect for the right of all and each.

Justice is the guardian of order and, consequently, of peace. Without justice, men would always be fighting like wild beasts over the prey. Hence the Biblical saying: *"Opus justitiae pax"*—"The work of justice shall be peace." (*Is.* 32:17).

Without justice it is possible to have a purely external, mechanical, apparent, unstable order, liable to be broken with every wind that blows; and order resting on the points of bayonets.

One may recall the famous phrase of that French minister who, when asked in parliament concerning conditions in Poland, which had just been subjugated by the French army, replied: *"Order reigns in Warsaw."* In truth, Warsaw, the capital of Poland, was completely under the heel of the invaders: it was a purely external order that prevailed, and so they called it *"the order of Warsaw."* The phrase of the French minister re-echoed the famous saying of the writer Tacitus: *"Ubi solitudinem faciunt pacem appellant"*—"They have made a wilderness and they call it peace."

But Christian peace, true peace, is neither wilderness nor helplessness, nor stillness; that is the peace of cemeteries. Christian peace is life, it is motion, it is spontaneous action, the fruit of harmony and cooperation.

There is an *inward peace* that reigns among men's faculties, whereby the lower are subject to the higher; and there is an *outward peace* that reflects the relations between man and man, between classes, and between peoples. Outward peace is *national* when the relations between rulers and subjects and between citizens are founded on justice. It is *international* when the relations between nations that make up the human family are founded on justice.

We now wish to examine the *prerogatives of Christian peace*, but in order to do this we must first know *the examples and the teachings of Christ concerning peace.*

The Examples and Teachings of Christ

1. Jesus Christ was foretold by the prophets as the Bearer of Peace, the Peaceful King.

Isaias says: "And he shall judge the Gentiles, and rebuke many people; and they shall turn their swords into plowshares, and their spears into sickles; nation shall not lift up sword against nation, neither shall they be exercised any more to war." (*Is.* 2:4). The Kingdom of Christ will, therefore, be the Kingdom of Peace; the same prophet, in fact, elsewhere calls the future Messias the *Prince of Peace.* (*Is.* 9:6).

Zacharias, the father of the Baptist, prophesied that the Divine Messias will come "to enlighten them that sit in darkness and in the shadow of death, to direct our feet into the way of peace." (*Lk.* 1:79).

The prophecies find their fulfillment in the doctrine,

in the teachings and in the life of Christ.

2. First of all in the *teachings of Christ.*

Around the cradle the angels proclaim: *"Peace to men of good will."* It is the first and only wish that Heaven sends to earth upon the appearance of the Saviour, but are not all other wishes included in it?

Jesus made a summary of His public teachings by His Sermon on the Mount, which is, as it were, His program, and in it He said: "Blessed are the peacemakers, for they shall be called the children of God." (*Matt.* 5:9). And the peacemakers in this case are those who are at peace with their brethren. They are called by the honorable title of *Sons of God,* because the Lord, as St. Paul says, is the *God of Peace.* (*2 Cor.* 13:11).

Peace is the loving wish of Jesus to His disciples: "Have peace among you." (*Mk.* 9:49). It is the legacy, the only legacy which He leaves to them in the discourse of the Last Supper, which is, as it were, His last will: "Peace I leave with you, my peace I give to you, not as the world giveth do I give to you." (*Jn.* 14:27). And His first word of greeting to them after the Ressurection is: *"Pax vobis."*—"Peace be to you." (*Jn.* 20:19).

Besides, He wants His disciples to be messengers of peace: "And when you come into the house, salute it . . . If that house be worthy, your peace shall come upon it." (*Matt.* 10:12-13).

However, there is a passage in the Gospel that seems to be in conflict with the practical mission of the Saviour. In fact, He said: "Do not think that I came to send peace upon earth: I came not to send peace, but the sword." (*Matt.* 10:34).

Some who know no other passages from the Gospel but this claim that Jesus is in favor of war. These persons do not understand the true meaning of these words. Jesus speaks of that ceaseless war that the Christian must wage against the enemies of good, with spiritual and unbloody means. It is not the sort of war, therefore, that sows the battlefields of the earth with corpses, but that which fills Heaven with souls; it is the war that is waged by the martyrs dying in their own blood unshaken.

3. Furthermore, against this materialistic interpretation are not only the *teachings*, but the whole *life* of Christ. Jesus made His solemn entry into Jerusalem riding, not on a fiery charger, but on a meek and lowly donkey. Why? The Evangelist tells us: so that what the prophet foretold might be fulfilled: "Behold thy king cometh to thee, meek and sitting upon an ass." (*Matt.* 21:5).

The Jews were dreaming that the Messias would be a warrior, and a conqueror: Jesus presents Himself to them as a mild King, as the Prince of Peace.

When the inhabitants of a Samaritan city had refused Him hospitality, two of His disciples, James and John, prompted by an indiscreet zeal, put this question to Him: "Lord, wilt thou that we command fire to come down from heaven and consume them?" and Jesus replied: "You know not of what spirit you are; for the Son of Man did not come to destroy souls, but to save." (*Lk.* 9:54-56).

During His arrest in the Garden of Olives, Peter, in order to defend his Master, drew his sword and cut off the ear of Malchus, the servant of the high priest, but Jesus rebuked him thus: "Put up again thy sword into its place, for all that take the sword shall perish with the sword." (*Matt.* 26:51-52).

The conclusion is obvious: Christ did bring the sword upon earth, but not that of Peter that kills; His is a spiritual sword that kills not, but quickens.

The Prerogatives of Christian Peace

What are the prerogatives of the peace of Christ, of that peace that He brought to the world and that He wills should reign at all times and in all places, in individual, family and social life among men and nations?

In substance, the peace of Christ is friendship with God and with men: first of all, *inward* peace, from which, as rays from the sun, comes *outward* peace; peace within souls, from which it *radiates upon things;* peace *founded on justice* and *inspired by charity.*

Let us develop these two doctrines:

1. *Peace founded on justice.*

Jesus came upon earth not only to *preach peace,* but to *bring justice,* which is the *foundation* and the *safeguard* of peace, as we have seen. The prophet Isaias, speaking of the future Redeemer, says with a poetic phrase, "And justice shall be the girdle of his loins." (*Is.* 6:5). And the Psalmist, describing the work of the Messias, exclaimed: "Justice and peace have kissed." (*Ps.* 84:11).

How Christ inculcated justice, the basic virtue of individual and social life, we have already seen in Chapter VI. His disciples must not only "hunger and thirst after justice" (*Matt.* 5:6), but they must be ready to suffer every kind of persecution rather than default in their duties toward justice. In fact, the last Beatitude runs thus: "Blessed are they that suffer persecution for justice' sake, for theirs is the kingdom of heaven." (*Matt.* 5:10).

2. *The peace of Christ is not, therefore, any peace whatever, peace at any cost.* It is peace founded on justice; therefore, when justice is violated and there is no other means of redressing it, it is lawful to have recourse to *force,* which is entirely different from violence, since it is not summoned to the service of caprice or of passions (like violence), but of law and order. Hence, the *lawfulness of war* under certain circumstances.

According to Catholic moralists, war is lawful when:

(a) *It is declared by legitimate authority;*

(b) It is just; that is, is waged for a just motive, such as re-establishing justice when offended, repairing an injury or defending oneself against aggression;

(c) *It is inevitable;* that is, when all other peaceful means of obtaining justice and of obtaining redress have failed;

(d) *It is useful;* insofar as it is likely that the advantages obtained will outweigh the damages suffered.

Some pacifists accuse the religion of Christ with legalizing war which, according to them, is never lawful. It should be pointed out to these people that justice is a higher good than peace itself, because without justice, as already observed, there can be no human society. That accounts for the coining of the aphorism: *"fiat justitia, pereat mundus"*—let justice be done, though the world should perish!

In the second place it is to be noted that the religion of Christ, by condemning every injustice, thereby condemns and at the same time seeks to do away with every cause of war, for most wars, as we know, are nothing but acts of violence and abuses of power.

3. *Christian peace, besides being founded on justice, is inspired by charity.*

As a matter of fact, it is difficult to observe the rules of justice if there is no fire of charity burning in the heart. Indeed, charity is the inspirer, the nourisher, the guardian of peace. If men love themselves like brothers, they cannot offend or kill one another as enemies.

The peace of Christ was promised by the heavenly messengers to *"men of good will";* and the will is good precisely when it is guided by justice and inspired by love.

The Prophet Isaias saw and described this wonderful scene in the future reign of Christ: "The wolf and the lamb shall feed together, the lion and ox shall eat straw." (*Is.* 65:25).

What will ever be able to achieve this prodigy, that those who are wont to tear each other to pieces should become friends? The love of Christ. Take away this love and that which a cynical philosopher fancied concerning the origin of society will readily come true: *"homo homini lupus"*—"Man is a wolf to man."

The representatives of all nations have been seeking and are still seeking a way to general disarmament, or at least to substantial reduction of arms. *Physical disarmament* is an excellent thing, but either it will never come to pass, or it will not last unless it is preceded and accompanied by *moral disarmament:* that is the disarmament of spirits, stripped of every feeling of hatred, of vengeance, of individual and collective selfishness.

Peace is sometimes represented by an angel bearing an olive branch in its hands. This angel of peace soars aloft on two wings, the names of which are *justice* and *love.*

The Teachings of the Popes

1. The Popes, the representatives of the Prince of Peace, have not only invoked peace and deplored war, but they have also pointed out the ways of peace—namely, the means and the methods of achieving and of preserving it.

This salutary teaching is found repeatedly in the writings of recent Popes, who have seen the horror and the ruin of the last world wars. They are Benedict XV, Pius XI and Pius XII. They pointed out particularly the foundations and the safeguards of peace, in the following remedies: *association of nations, universal disarmament, compulsory arbitration* (for the solution of international controversies), *the independence of all nations, respect of minorities,* and *equitable distribution of wealth* (among the various nations, large and small, rich and poor).

We will confine ourselves to a few citations:

2. Benedict XV, *in his note to the heads of belligerent nations* (August 1, 1917) wrote: "First of all, the fundamental point must be that the moral force of right shall be substituted for the material force of arms; thence must follow a just agreement of all for the *simultaneous* and *reciprocal diminution of armaments,* in accordance with rules and guarantees to be established hereafter, in a measure sufficient and necessary for the maintenance of public order in each State; next, as a substitute for armies, the *institution* of *arbitration,* with its high peace-making function, subject to

regulations to be agreed on and sanctions to be determined against the State which should refuse either to submit international questions to arbitration or to accept its decision."

The same Pontiff, in the Encyclical *Pacem Dei Munus* (May 23, 1920) said: "It is much to be desired, Venerable Brethren, that all States, putting aside mutual suspicion should unite in one society, or rather a single family calculated both to maintain their own indepedence and safeguard the order of human society. What specially, among other reasons, calls for such an association of nations, is the need generally recognized of making every effort to abolish or reduce the enormous burden of the military expenditures which States can no longer bear, in order to prevent these disastrous wars or at least to remove the danger of them as far as possible. So would each nation be assured not only of its own independence but also of the integrity of its territory within its just frontiers."

3. Pius XII, in his discourse of Dec. 24, 1939, on the requisites for a just and honorable peace said, among other things:

"A fundamental postulate of any just and honorable peace *is an assurance for all nations, great or small, powerful or weak, of their right to life and independence.* The will of one nation to live must never mean the sentence of death passed upon another. When this equality of rights has been destroyed, attacked or threatened, order demands that reparation shall be made, and the measure and extent of that reparation is determined, not by the sword nor by arbitrary decision of self-interest, but by the rules of justice and reciprocal equity.

"The order thus established, if it is to continue undisturbed and ensure true peace, requires *that the nations be delivered from the slavery imposed upon them by the race for armaments;* and from the danger that material force, instead of serving to protect the right, may become an overbearing and tyrannical master. Any peaceful settlement that fails to give fundamental importance to a mutually agreed, organic and progressive disarmament, spiritual as well as material, or which neglects to ensure the effective and loyal implementing of such an agreement, will sooner or later show itself to be lacking in coherence and vitality."

The same Pontiff, in his broadcast of December 24, 1951, set forth the bases of a just and lasting peace and stated that:

"Within the limits of a new order founded on moral principles, there is no place for that cold and calculating egoism which tends to hoard economic resources and materials destined for the use of all, to such an extent that the nations less favored by nature are not permitted access to them. In this regard, it is a source of great consolation to see admitted the necessity of a participation of all in the natural riches of the earth even on the part of those nations which, in the fulfillment of this principle, belong to the category of givers and not to that of receivers. It is, however, in conformity with the principles of equity that a solution to a question so vital to the world economy should be arrived at methodically, and in easy stages, with a necessary guarantee, always drawing useful lessons from the omissions and mistakes of the past. If, in the future peace, this point were not to be courageously dealt with, there would remain in the relations between people a deep and far-reaching root blossoming forth into bitter dissensions and burning jealousies, which would lead eventually to new conflicts.

"The maxims of human wisdom require that in any reorganization of international life all parties should learn a lesson from the failures and deficiencies of the past. Hence, in creating or reconstructing international institutions which have so high a mission and such difficult and grave responsibilities, it is important to bear in mind the experience gained from the ineffectiveness or imperfections of previous institutions of the kind."

The exhortation of Christ to His disciples, an exhortation that is also command: *"Have peace among you" (Mk.* 9:49), still re-echoes in the heart-rending words of the representatives of Christ. That exhortation is addressed also to us: Let us keep peace in our own little world; in our family, in our society, in our place of work, in our community, in the circle of our friends and acquaintances. Away with animosities, with quarrels, with envy!

Let us hearken to the appeal of the Apostle: "If it be possible, as much as is in you, have peace with all men." (*Rom.* 12:18).

Let us strive to be at peace with all men, even if all around us there is hatred and strife. Thus we will help to bring about the peace of Christ—universal peace!

If you have enjoyed this book, consider making your next selection from among the following . . .

At your bookdealer or direct from the publisher.

Prices guaranteed through December 31, 1992.